T.S. Eliot

Collected Poems

1909-1962

L'auteur

Helen Goethals est professeur honoraire à l'université Toulouse-Jean Jaurès et membre fondateur du Laboratoire Ouvert de l'Œuvre Poétique (LOOP). Elle a publié *The Unassuming Sky: The Life and Poetry of Timothy Corsellis* (2012), *In Various Light: Tributes to Derek Walcott, 1930-2017* (avec Eric Doumerc, 2022), ainsi que de nombreux articles sur les relations entre poésie et politique.

La collection *Clefs-concours Anglais – Littérature* est dirigée par

Élisabeth Soubrenie.

Direction scientifique des *Clefs-concours* : **Philippe Lemarchand**.

Édition : Lucille Fontaine.
Mise en pages : Anouk Grandjean.

ISBN : 978-2-35030-919-4

CLEFS-CONCOURS ANGLAIS – LITTÉRATURE

Helen Goethals

T.S. Eliot
Collected Poems 1909-1962

Atlande

CONTENTS

CONTEXTS

ANALYSIS

NOTE

Numbers in parentheses refer to the recommended edition of the *Collected Poems*.

'See' + a title links to a chapter in this book.

An asterisk after a word* means that the word will be found in the glossary.

ACKNOWLEDGEMENTS

> The reader should be carried forward, not merely or chiefly by the mechanical impulse of curiosity,
> not by a restless desire to arrive at the final solution, but by the pleasurable activity of the journey itself.
>
> —S.T. Coleridge, *Biographia Literaria* (1817)

Reading poetry, especially modern poetry, has offered me delight and wisdom ever since I was able to read. For what was the first book that I was ever given to read? Why, Dr. Seuss's *The Cat in the Hat* (1957) of course. On what I like to imagine as a quest for a meaning that is not quixotic, there have been many people who have offered guidance along the way, and some of these I would like to acknowledge here.

The first is Jane Higgs, whose teaching of T.S. Eliot's *Selected Poems* (1948), one of the books set for 'A' level, was inspirational. Although she was clearly under the spell of the work of **Helen Gardner**, under whom she had read English at St. Hilda's, Oxford, she gave us no literary criticism to read whatsoever. Nothing but the text and B.C. Southam's *Student's Guide*, "an aid, to be used like any dictionary or work of reference, to be consulted and then put aside". The 'first fine careless rapture' of that direct encounter with Eliot now seems a world away:

> What was the modern movement in English and American literature has now passed into history. We have to call it the 'modernist movement'. Its great figures—Yeats, Pound, Eliot, Joyce, Lawrence, Wallace Stevens—are now well entrenched in academic syllabuses. The vultures and the crows have moved in over the old battlefields. Writers who once aroused a passionate enthusiasm and as passionate a disapproval are now the prey of bibliographers and textual critics, biographers and editors of letters, and students seeking doctorates. [GARDNER, 1982, p. 12]

In fact, it is to the very 'textual critic' that Gardner had in mind that I owe the most: **Christopher Ricks**. For the first trimester of the course he personally designed at Bristol University we read nothing but John

Hayward's *Penguin Book of English Verse* (1958). Happily, and uncoincidentally, John Hayward's idea of an English tradition was also Eliot's. As well as Christopher Ricks' writing on Eliot (see "Bibliography"), I was later to be much influenced by his defence of what, after Dr. Johnson, he called "literary principles". These he set against the "literary theory" which long dominated the English departments of French and American universities. "A fully-fledged theory, taking wing, is a philosophy; a fully compacted principle is rooted as a proverb." [Ricks, 1996, p. 323].

The reading of modern English poetry at the University of Lyon II, where I studied and then taught, was dominated by the convivial presence of **Adolphe Haberer**. Though I was not able to share his Lacanian approach to poetry, I admired, then and now, the spirit of his textual analysis and, adapted to my own more contextualized and comparative approach, it is his organization of close reading that I have followed in this study. To read a poem requires patience as well as passion, letting the meaning of the poem slowly emerge, in its own good time. It is only after one has methodically observed the precise semiotics, sounds, syntax, semantics and stylistic devices of the text, that one can begin to understand the something "almost being said" in poetry [Larkin, 1988, p. 166]. The scholarly and sympathetic spirit of such readings continues today in the online gatherings and conferences of the members of the Laboratoire Ouvert de l'Œuvre Poétique (LOOP).

Finally, in a study focused on the reader, it is only right to acknowledge the particular readership for whom it has been written. Many readers are daunted by poetry in general and reputedly difficult modern poetry in particular. I would from the outset like to take the opportunity to reassure the *agrégatifs* that they are not alone. As long ago as 1936, the editor of *The Faber Book of Modern Verse* —with *The Waste Land* as its centerpiece— was already writing ruefully:

> More often than prose or mathematics, poetry is received in a hostile spirit, as if its publication were an affront to the reader; yet most of the poetry which is published probably appears because it delighted the writer and convinced him that it held some profound significance or some exact description which he hoped that others, too, might see. [Roberts, 1936, p. 1]

Others have been there before us: let us take heart together and as Eliot (198), after the Bhagavad-Gita, once said, *Not fare well, / But fare forward voyagers*.

FOREWORD

Let us go then, you and I,
When the evening is spread out against the sky
Like a patient etherised upon a table; (3)

For self-evident reasons of time and space, this discussion of T.S. Eliot's poetry will be confined to the 34 poems set for the *agrégation d'anglais*. I suggest that we begin by taking a stroll, quite literally, through the pages of the *Collected Poems*. Let us consider what light (or shadow) is cast by the immediate, material context, also known as the paratext*, on the poems that have been chosen for us to read. The following discussion, and all references to the poems, refer to the latest printing of the edition, which has not changed since 1963.

That the poems are presented to us, as it were, in a plain brown wrapper is suggestive in two ways. On the one hand, that plainness is typical of poetry books, the covers of which are rarely enticing: the idea is that poetry is so heady that it should be sampled neat, with no frills or frippery. Introductions, or notes, or any other form of reader-friendly paratext, are often, as here, conspicuously absent. This somewhat Puritanical attitude towards poetry is further reinforced by the categorical sign "Poetry" stamped —is it a trigger-warning?— on the right-hand corner of both the front and the back covers. On the other hand, the editor's choice of colour for the cover amusingly subverts the chaste exterior: for plain brown wrappers are traditionally used to allow the postal delivery of sexually explicit magazines and so, by extension, are used as a mask for what is considered disturbing content. In the case of Eliot, this might be a wise precaution: one reader, returning to *The Waste Land* after many years, remarked that he was surprised to find there was so much sex in it.

On the front cover we read the author's name, "T.S. Eliot", and the contents on offer: *Collected Poems 1909-1962*. *What's in a name? A rose by any other name would smell as sweet*. When Romeo famously asks that question, his answer leaves so much more to be said. Indeed, one Modernist writer began to say it: *Rose is a rose is a rose* (Stein 189). 'Rose', we note, is a common and a proper noun. While both types of nouns are only arbitrary and agreed signs, working as convenient symbols for something other than themselves, yet there is an important difference between them. As Romeo was to learn to his cost, associations cling more closely to proper nouns than to common ones. A family name bears the weight of the history of that family, sometimes unto the third and fourth generation. The poem "Cousin Nancy" (22), for example, plays with the contrast between the fictionalized name "Miss Nancy Ellicott" and the deceptively playful references to "Matthew and Waldo", while remaining careful to avoid the unmentionable common nouns at the heart of the poem: 'tomboy' and 'nancy-boy'.

It is worth pausing on the initials "T.S.". In the nineteenth-century this was a ploy used by women-writers, such as the Brontë sisters, as a way of forestalling the prejudice of readers and editors. The practice has become less common in modern times, though there are important exceptions: A.E. Stallings, the present Oxford Professor of Poetry, is one example. In Eliot's time, did he have anything in common with these poets who were contemporaries of his: A.E. Housman, 'A.E.' and 'H.D.'?

In ordinary life, Eliot was almost universally known as 'Tom', not 'T.S.'. Doubtless, he wished to make a characteristic and useful distinction between the man and the poet. Later in life, he was known by the junior staff at the Faber offices (among whom, his future second wife, Valerie Fletcher) as 'TSE'. The senior partners of the publishing firm, on the other hand, gave him a nickname: 'Old Possum', after the animal that escaped from awkward situations by becoming completely still and playing dead, from the Br'er Rabbit stories that Pound and Eliot used to read in their childhood.

Here would be a good place to pause and consider an idea that might be pursued by those who find a Lacanian approach to literature helpful. While bearing in mind that in a poem it is not Eliot himself speaking to us directly, but a persona*, nevertheless, even those unsympathetic to a psychoanalytical reading of poetry will find it difficult to ignore completely the Lacanian undertones of the following lines from "Portrait of a Lady":

> Among the windings of the violins
> And the ariettes
> Of cracked cornets
> Inside my brain a dull tom-tom begins
> Absurdly hammering a prelude of its own,
> Capricious monotone
> That is at least one definite 'false note.' (9)

The onomatopoeia* of 'tom-tom' is striking, and Eliot elsewhere elaborates on the origins of poetry in the jungle drumbeat:

> Poetry begins, I dare say, with a savage beating a drum in a jungle, and it retains that essential of percussion and rhythm. [ELIOT, 1933, p. 155]

But 'tom-tom' is also a play on the poet's own name. 'Tom', indeed, lends itself to many variations of the Lacanian theme of names being more than they seem. Consider, at your own discretion, the non-exhaustive list set in motion by 'tom-tom': tomboy, tomcat, tomfoolery, every Tom, Dick and Harry, Tommy Atkins, tommyrot, Tom O'Bedlam, Tom Thumb…

"*Collected Poems 1909-1962*," writes critic Hugh Haughton, "embodies one of the most complete and cunningly contrived oeuvres in the twentieth century." [HAMILTON, 1994, p. 149]. To put it more bluntly, this collection is less complete and more contrived than it might at first seem. The term 'collected' indicates the poet's own selection from his work, all that he wishes to preserve for posterity, a decision that can vary according to what the poet is still writing and what, retrospectively, he or she is best pleased with at the time of selection. In the case of modern poets such as Robert Graves or W.H. Auden, for example, such variables can result in a whole series of different Collected Poems, and a nightmare for bibliographers. Fortunately, this is not the case with Eliot, whose collections proceeded, from 1925 through 1936 to the final and present collection of 1963, in orderly fashion and by apparently simple accretion.

The various slim volumes have been arranged in the chronological order of their publication (1917, 1920, 1922, 1925, 1930). These are followed by the five 'Ariel' poems originally published annually as illustrated pamphlets intended as Christmas presents. Two 'Unfinished Poems' complete the number of poems we are required to study. We may surmise that the choice of poems for the *agrégation* syllabus was made as dispassionately as Eliot himself might have wished, since it mathematically reduces the number of pages (130 out of 216) to be studied by drawing a clear chronological line through the Table of Contents.

The main effect, of course, is that our 34 poems are severed from Eliot's other 'famous poem', *Four Quartets*. Since these are the culmination of Eliot's poetic *oeuvre*, it seems willful not to read the poems which come before them as in many ways leading up to this final work. This I think is true whatever one thinks of the *Quartets* themselves. Opinions on Eliot's last substantial poem are divided. Once again, Hugh Haughton puts the matter in a nutshell: "For some readers this [*Four Quartets*] represents the climax of Eliot's poetic *oeuvre*: for others, its anti-climactic betrayal." [Hamilton, 1994, p. 148]. Perhaps those who set the syllabus incline to the latter view?

If we set aside "The Cultivation of Christmas Trees", this means that we shall be looking only at poems written between 1909 and 1930: the twenty-or-so years stretching from Eliot's twenty-first birthday to that of his forty-second. Seen in literary terms, and retrospectively, Eliot's private progress from youth to middle age corresponds to the literary period which is often described as the heyday of Modernism*. We shall have more to say about this important but not unproblematic parallel later (see A Sketch of an Age).

What has been collected here is by no means all the poetry that T.S. Eliot wrote. Readers who are curious about what Eliot chose *not* to collect, are now able to consult the near-definitive edition of T.S. Eliot's work meticulously compiled in two weighty volumes by Christopher Ricks and Jim McCue. Volume One contains *Collected Poems 1910-1962*, Uncollected Poems, an editorial composite of *The Waste Land*, and a commentary. Volume Two (available online from Internet Archive) contains *Old Possum's Book of Practical Cats*, *Anabasis*, Other Verses, Noctes Binanianae, Improper Rhymes, a commentary, and a note on textual history. For the 34 poems on the syllabus, it is sometimes useful to be aware of what Eliot was writing *at the same time* as our selection. The *Collected Poems* have been carefully chosen and very formally arranged: what happens to our reading of them if they are read alongside the rejected poems, light verse, verse in translation, and lewd verse?

The same is true of *The Waste Land*. We are not required to study the 'editorial composite' but it is helpful to know that it exists. Ricks' version is a presentation of the poem as Eliot first wrote it, complete with the passages excised and annotated by Eliot, Ezra Pound, Vivien and others. The original manuscript only came to light after Eliot's death; it was his second wife Valerie who had the original draft published, in 1971. What we read in the *Collected Poems* is the abridged version, published in 1922.

The long list of works "By T.S. Eliot" opposite the title page helps to remind us of the many kinds of writing by Eliot that we are not, strictly speaking, required to read, beginning with the five plays that Eliot wrote between 1935 and 1958. Nevertheless, their very existence suggests two remarks that are pertinent to our 34 poems. First, we may note that Eliot's style of playwriting moved from a prewar interest in experimental theatre to the more conventional comedy of manners* of the post-war period. Secondly, if we set aside the exceptional wartime writing of the *Four Quartets*, Eliot moved *from* the writing of poetry *to* the writing of plays, from one genre to another. This is what makes the last two poems on the syllabus, "Sweeney Agonistes" and "Corialan", particularly interesting. They are classed by Eliot himself as "unfinished poems", but could it not be argued that they are unfinished because they were not so much the first drafts of poems as of plays? Certainly, some have thought so, and these 'poems' have occasionally been performed as plays. We are not required to look at the poetic qualities of the plays, nor to consider too deeply the function of 'verse drama', but it would be unwise not to think about the dramatic —perhaps even the theatrical— dimension of the poetry.

Secondly, we note that Eliot published a considerable amount of literary criticism, partly for reasons that will be discussed in the next chapter. Meanwhile, we can make a few general about the criticism of a poet, as opposed to that of a full-time critic. First, a poet's criticism is worth reading because it is usually very well-written, almost surprisingly so, given how many poets profess to a dislike of writing in prose. Second, it does often give useful insights into the poet's ideas about the nature and function of poetry in general, and for that reason, we will make abundant use of choice quotations from the essays. Although they fall well outside our period, the two essays of 'social criticism', *The Idea of a Christian Society* and *Notes towards a Definition of Culture*, as their very titles suggest, offer illuminating perspectives on the rest of the work. Finally, certain of the essays were written and published in parallel to the poetry. The idea that the prose of *The Sacred Wood* is an indispensable accompaniment to the poetry of *The Waste Land*, for example, is a theme that will underpin our later argument.

Let us conclude our survey of the *Collected Poems* with the most cursory of readings, in order to see what can be understood merely by contemplating the words on the page, without seeking to understand them, as though they were written in a foreign language which we neither know nor seek to know. For those who read almost exclusively plain prose, such a deliberately shallow reading might at first seem odd, perhaps even meaningless but, as will be explained later, in poetry it is a vital first step, an invitation to share each artist's particular way of looking at the world:

> Art was given for that;
> God uses us to help each other so
> Lending our minds out.
> (Robert Browning, "Fra Lippo Lippi")

So, what can we observe simply by thumbing through the 130 pages of words aligned to look like poems? Three observations stand out. First, our selection encompasses a wide variety of verse forms. One form, however, is conspicuous by its absence: the sonnet. Why that should be so is a question worth pondering. Setting aside the anomalous 'unfinished poems', what we *do* have are 12 short, single-stanza poems occupying a single page. 13 other poems are arranged in stanzas and take up two pages. Seven of the 13 stanza-poems are actually in quatrains; this is surprising, since the quatrain is a traditional and popular form, and not one associated with the Modernists. The poems which have the most unusual form are 8 long poems. These are divided into irregular sections, with the divisions sometimes marked by Roman numerals, sometimes by a line-space, sometimes by dots. The divisions divide the poem into thematic sections, often, though not always, called verse paragraphs*.

Another feature which is striking at first glance is the irregularity of the line-length. This can range from the line of one word/one syllable, the 'But' in "A Game of Chess" (57) to the 13 words/16 syllables in "Gerontion" (30), in a line so long that it requires to be dropped*:

> The tiger springs in the new year. Us he devours. Think at
> last

In modern verse, the layout is part of the meaning. Indeed, one characteristic of Modernist verse is that it was primarily written for the page. Another characteristic is that its auditory elements, those that appeal to the ear, are muted and need to be compensated, if the poem is to have any unity at all, by elements that appeal to the eye. In 1927 poets Laura Riding and Robert Graves proclaimed, in *A Survey of Modernist Poetry*, that free verse is free only in the limited —albeit liberating— sense of being 'self-determining':

> Modern poetry, that is, is groping for some principle of self-determination to be applied to the making of the poem — not lack of government but government from within. [Riding, 1928, p. 27]

In other words, it is the content which determines the form, not the other way around (as formerly, in a ballad for instance). Form itself is freed to become signifying. This phenomenon can be likened to what the art critic Clive Bell called significant form*, and it means that every layout, especially an unusual one, is intentional on the part of the author, and so its effects can only be considered in terms of the context of the poem. There are no hard and fast rules. In the case of a 'mixed poem', such as the quatrain poems, we need to think *both* about what the traditional form can do, about why he chooses to use that form, *and* how and why he modernizes it.

Secondly, we observe that the collection contains prose as well as poetry. "Hysteria" is a prose-poem*, modelled on Baudelaire's "Petits poèmes en prose" (1869) and its apparent subject may well be related to Baudelaire's famous declaration:

> J'ai cultivé mon hystérie avec jouissance et terreur. Maintenant j'ai toujours le vertige, et aujourd'hui, 23 janvier 1862, j'ai subi un singulier avertissement, j'ai senti passer sur moi le vent de l'aile de l'imbécillité. [Baudelaire, 2001, p. 668]

The Modernists generally were interested in the newness of the prose-poem as a genre, and the single example that we find in Eliot's collection is worth reading in the light of other Modernist work. In "Blue and Green" for example, Virginia Woolf presents us with a short story which can also be read as a magnificent prose-poem. Ernest Hemingway, another great Modernist, was later to make brilliant use of the modern prose-poem form in the 18 vignettes of *in our time* (1924). The only other pages in prose (70-76) in *Collected Poems* are the "Notes on The Waste Land". Critics disagree over how far these notes are to be taken seriously but none can deny that they form an innovative and therefore controversial appendix to the poem.

And thirdly, we observe that for such a towering figure of Modernism, and despite what we said above, Eliot uses relatively few visual innovations. All the poems have titles*. All the lines begin with capital letters. This makes the very few exceptions to this traditional layout (on pages 58 and 63, for example) all the more interesting. This visual sobriety sets Eliot apart from Pound, with his fondness for Chinese ideograms, and from e.e. cummings, with his use of the lower case and the hyphen. How should we interpret Eliot's limited interest in the visual sign? Perhaps we could relate it to the idea, which we might not want to push too far, that the modern, the experimental component in Eliot's poems has less to do with typographical experimentation and more to do with musical arrangement of words on a page and the introduction of new —really new— sounds. Perhaps Eliot's 'intelligent sensibility' was more akin to that of the John Cage of 4'33 than to the artwork of, say, Fernand Léger?

In sum, this *état des lieux* has served to draw attention to the commercial (which is also the social and the cultural) side of the publishing of poetry. This material aspect of our reading the "words on the page" is rarely explored, except by those few scholars interested in New Literary History, but it *is* relevant to Eliot, a poet who was both a publisher committed to increasing the sale of poetry books and a Modernist with strong ideas about the need to improve the relationship between the artist and their audience. Read literally and from a distance, *Collected Poems,* the book, offers an implicit statement about the nature and function of poetry as Eliot saw them: in a finite world, poetry should be set, if not above, then at least apart from prose and verse drama, and some kinds of poems should be set apart from others, according to their intended audience. Since Eliot's presuppositions about how poetry should be read were carried into practice, and have largely become our own, we shall go on to examine them a little more closely in the next chapter.

INTRODUCTION: THE ART OF READING

> I rejoice to concur with the common reader; for by the common sense of readers, uncorrupted by literary prejudices, after all the refinements of subtlety and the dogmatism of learning, must finally be decided all claims to poetical honours.
> — Dr. Johnson, *Life of Gray* (1779)

In 1925, Virginia Woolf entitled her first published series of essays *The Common Reader*, a figure which she borrowed from Dr. Johnson, and whom she described thus:

> He reads for his own pleasure rather than to impart knowledge or correct the opinions of others. Above all, he is guided by an instinct to create for himself, out of whatever odds and ends he can come by, some kind of whole — a portrait of a man, a sketch of an age, a theory of the art of writing. He never ceases, as he reads, to run up some rickety and ramshackle fabric which shall give him the temporary satisfaction of looking sufficiently like the real object to allow of affection, laughter, and argument. [WOOLF, 1925, p. 11-12]

If we set aside the pronoun 'he' —regrettable, but no doubt unavoidable in the 1920s and, coming from Woolf, not entirely lacking in irony— and ignoring the fact that she was primarily interested in the reader of novels, then we are left with a type of reader with whom we might all feel at ease. Nearly one hundred years later, this 'common reader' continues to correspond to our own reading experience "guided by an instinct to create for himself, out of whatever odds and ends he can come by, some kind of whole". [Woolf, 1925, p. 12]

The "odds and ends" that *agrégation* candidates bring to the experience of reading poetry are by no means negligible: critical tools, historical background and (above all) a solid grounding in linguistics. A firm grasp of how and why grammar works in the way it does helps us to understand the effects of the poet's conformity, or deliberate lack of conformity, to the conventional rules of prose. Reading poetry requires us to refine what we have learnt through the study of phonetics, pragmatics, and the question of performative* language. Students will find the course on Puritanism by no means irrelevant to understanding Eliot's religious thinking, and those already reading *Hamlet*, will recognize the allusion* in this excerpt from "The Love-Song of J. Alfred Prufrock":

> No! I am not Prince Hamlet nor was meant to be;
> Am an attendant lord, one that will do
> To swell a progress, start a scene or two,
> Advise the prince; no doubt; an easy tool,
> Deferential, glad to be of use,
> Politic, cautious, and meticulous;
> Full of high sentence, but a bit obtuse;
> At times, almost ridiculous –
> Almost, at times, the Fool. (7)

Such readers are more likely to pick up even fainter echoes of the Shakespeare play, as in this excerpt from "Portrait of a Lady":

> And I must borrow every changing shape
> To find expression … dance, dance
> Like a dancing bear,
> Cry like a parrot, chatter like an ape. (11)

Who is the Fool in Hamlet? What does it mean to put on an 'antic disposition' (Hamlet 1, 5)? Whether we treat these lines as allusion or intertextuality* (see Allusion) the *rapprochement* works both ways, illuminating the source text as well as its rewriting. *Agrégatifs* will be able to question Eliot's reference to the lack of an objective correlative*, not only in relation to *Hamlet,* but also in relation to Eliot's own poems. What use does Eliot make, or not make, of an objective correlative in his own poems, and to what effect? In "The Hollow Men", for example?

The problem is not that the common reader has too little knowledge but that we have too much and that we are not sure how to *organize* what we have into "some kind of whole". As we shall see, poetry helps us to do just that. In the words of Robert Frost, "the initial delight is in the surprise of remembering something that I didn't know I knew" [HERBERT, 2000, p. 45]. The delight might not come at the initial reading but if the poem *is* a poem, and we read for pleasure, come it will. A poem discloses its meaning slowly and so we must follow Walt Whitman's advice, reading and re-reading it, letting it linger on the tongue and in the ear, turning it over in our sensible minds, suffering the poem to come to us:

> Failing to fetch me at first keep me encouraged,
> Missing me one place search another,
> I stop somewhere waiting for you. [WHITMAN, 1973, p. 89]

THE NEW READING PUBLIC

If Virginia Woolf took such care to address her essays to the 'common reader', it was because she felt that the writing of literature had entered, once again, into a phase during which writers and readers found it difficult to understand each other. This was not a new phenomenon: the gap had been widening at least since 1800, when Wordsworth and Coleridge felt the new, and at the time astonishing, need to write a Preface to the second edition of their *Lyrical Ballads*. [ENRIGHT, 1962, pp. 162-189]. *Only connect*, said E.M. Forster; the crisis for the Modernists was one of *not* connecting with their 'New Reading Public', both those who had benefited from the Education Act of 1870 and, later, those who had lived in and survived the trenches of World War I. Literature had hitherto been largely dominated by a class which had had the leisure first to write, and then to read. But that class was seen as increasingly redundant, even parasitical, in a rapidly industrializing world which appeared to require only the material wealth produced by the working and middle classes who had no interest in reading. Writers were in a double bind. No longer *rentiers*, they found themselves in a literary marketplace in which they needed to please the unknown readers on whom they depended for a living. At the same time, it was up to them, as writers, to convince both classes that modern literature represented real value in a modern world.

Eliot certainly shared Woolf's anxieties about the status of the artist in the modern world, first as a writer who, unable to make a living from his writing, had to take on work which left him too exhausted to write and secondly as a critic invited to reflect on the relationship between poetry and criticism. In *The Use of Poetry and the Use of Criticism*, the eight lectures delivered at Harvard in the winter of 1932-33, Eliot's main contention was this:

> I suggest that we may learn a good deal about criticism and about poetry by examining the history of criticism, not merely as a catalogue of successive notions about poetry, but as a process of readjustment between poetry and the world in and for which it is produced. [ELIOT, 1933, p. 27]

Eliot's concern, it should be stressed, was not for the sociology of the writing and reading of poetry in general, but in the very particular historical predicament in which his generation found itself.

After pointing out that the poet-critic John Dryden (1631-1700) was unable to draw on the large and mixed audience that William Shakespeare (1564-1616) had enjoyed, Eliot goes on to say:

> But the part of society to which Dryden's work, and that of the restoration comedians, could immediately appeal, constituted something like an intellectual aristocracy; when the poet finds himself in an age in which there is no intellectual aristocracy, when power is in the hands of a class so democratized that whilst still a class it represents itself to be the whole nation; when the only alternatives seem to be to talk to a coterie or to soliloquize, the difficulties of the poet and the necessity of criticism become greater. [ELIOT, 1933, p. 22]

Eliot is here making the point that we suggested earlier: that literary criticism —in prefaces, manifestos, reviews— emerges when a poet's work is at odds with his immediate audience. But he is also implying some further points which we may need to bear in mind when we read the poems. First, he is clearly more in sympathy with the 'intellectual aristocracy', rather than the now all-powerful 'democratic class'.

Do these classes appear in his poems and, if so, how and in what relationship? Part of the answer to these questions may concern the terms tone* and voice*. Secondly, Eliot affirms that, for the modern poet who does not know who, if anyone, he is talking to, "the only alternatives seem to be to talk to a coterie* or to soliloquize". This affirmation begs several questions. Is it true? Are there no other ways to engage an invisible and potentially hostile audience? Can we classify all Eliot's poems (or parts of poems) as either dramatic monologues* "talking to a coterie" or soliloquies? Our answers to these questions will involve some notions of who, in the poem, is being addressed.

Eliot, like other Modernist writers, was very conscious of the difficulty of his writing. Further on in the same study, he considers the reasons for this difficulty. The four which he suggests are worth summarizing here. The reader's difficulty, he says, may be due to:

– personal causes which make it impossible for a poet to express himself in any but an obscure way
– the novelty of the writing
– the reader's expectation of difficulty (not stage fright but what Eliot calls "pit or gallery fright")
– the reader may be looking for a prose meaning which is not there

From our point of view, as critical as well as common readers, some knowledge of the poet's life (see A Portrait of a Poet) will elucidate the difficulties which arise from 'personal causes'. The question of 'novelty' is linked to what the Modernists felt to be the pressing concerns of their times, which will be dealt with in the "A Sketch of an Age" chapter. As for the reader's expectation of difficulty, we may note two things about Eliot's theatre metaphor. On the one hand, since the Elizabethan 'pit' has been replaced by the modern 'gallery' as the location of the cheapest theatre seats, Eliot implies that those who find modern poetry difficult are the poor; are we to understand that for the rich, in their theatre boxes, Eliot's poems are crystal-clear? On the other hand, and more interestingly, the metaphor betrays the persistent fusion in Eliot's mind of poetry and drama. Most telling of all, the expressions 'pit fright' and 'gallery fright', which he cannot quite bring himself to say, are delightfully performative in being a new combination of words for an old emotion (fear) in a new context (the modern theatre).

The Modernist writers were trying to say something *new*, something that had never been said before, and that they felt needed saying. If the audiences outside their own circle found their writing difficult simply because it was new, then those audiences would have to be educated. As has often been said, the Modernists in general and Eliot in particular were able to create and enlarge the audience by whom they wished to be read: both through the prose writing, in prefaces, manifestos, and articles in the 'little magazines' which proliferated at this time and, more excitingly, in the writing itself.

Taken out of context, the adjective 'common' in Virginia Woolf's 'common reader' could be confused with 'vulgar'. It is part of the dangerous charm of the Modernists that they tended to set themselves up as an 'intellectual aristocracy' who believed that their naturally fine writing and inherited good taste would gradually elevate the New Reading Public and redeem it from itself. Such a view was of course reactionary, and it had some very dark moments. As John Carey has shown, it is neither hard nor wrong to find in Modernist elitism many of the premises and prejudices of fascism. Indeed, so close to the wind do the Modernists sometimes steer that, in our own more censorious times, we would not be surprised to see the *Collected Poems* reissued with a trigger warning.

The more sunlit moments of Modernist writing are reminiscent of the *Belle Époque*, echoes of the many Impressionist paintings of the outdoor or open-window reader, who "reads for his own pleasure", "guided by his own instinct". Woolf's masculine pronouns are pleasantly attenuated by the fact that the Impressionist paintings in question are always of *female* readers. It was for just such an imaginary reader that the Modernists intended to write. To counter their own tendency to see the New Reading Public as a *public*, a mass, rather than as a number of diverse individuals, the Modernists at their best wrote in ways that by including actual, not idealized, readers could work towards creating their ideal 'common reader'. Faulkner's multiple points of view or Fernando Pessoa's heteronyms*, for example, can be seen as ways in which the Modernist author tries to efface his own social origins and perspective. T.S. Eliot brings together voices from every period, and from all walks of life, and the resultant shifts of register in his poems can be read as what we now call 'inclusive'. A supreme moment of Eliot's uncondescending and inclusionary attitude can be heard in the magnificent orchestration of voices at the end of "A Game of Chess" (59).

HURRY UP PLEASE ITS TIME
Well, that Sunday Albert was home, they had a hot gammon,
And they asked me to dinner, to get the beauty of it hot –
HURRY UP PLEASE ITS TIME
HURRY UP PLEASE ITS TIME
Goonight Bill. Goonight Lou. Goonight May. Goonight.
Ta ta. Goonight. Goonight.
Good night, ladies, good night, sweet ladies, good night,
 good night.

Eliot offers us a delightful medley of sounds. The voices of the Cockney drinkers and the publican calling time can be heard alongside the echoes of the Elizabethan poet Edmund Spenser and a music-hall song. Since Eliot ironically* excludes himself from the scene, it is up to us, the silent readers, to create a harmony out of this *discordia concors**. Astonished by the poet's virtuosity, we cannot help but hear both the sly innuendo* of 'hot', and the soft but persistent bass note of Time that reverberates throughout this section of *The Waste Land*.

As the above example shows —and only the effects of the words on the reader have been given here, not how those effects are achieved through typography, punctuation, spelling, grammar, repetition, allusion, and polysemy— the pleasure afforded by Modernist writing is certainly not that of *passive* reading. Unlike the traditional reader, the modern reader will have to become active. The compliment the Modernist writers paid to their readers by including them in their work, came at the price of reciprocal effort. *No tears for the writer, no tears for the reader. No surprise for the writer, no surprise for the reader*, warned Robert Frost [ENRIGHT, 1962, p. 45].

Enlisting an equal effort on the part of the reader as had already been made by the writer, the Modernists were unconsciously anticipating later theories about the 'Death of the Author'. T.S. Eliot's theory of impersonality* goes far beyond his particular desire to escape from his own personality in his work. It is an admission that, once the work was published, it no longer belonged to the poet, but became public property. And, throughout his life, Eliot professed himself willing to bear the consequences of this abdication from power:

> But what a poem means is as much what it means to others as what it means to the author; and indeed, in the course of time a poet may become merely a reader in respect to his own works, forgetting his original meaning — or without forgetting, merely changing. [ELIOT, 1933, p. 130]

Trust the poem, not the poet would therefore seem to be the surest of literary principles, for the writer as well as the reader.

ART AS EXPERIENCE

Naturally held back by the fact that they were *writers*, whose *raison d'être* was to write, most Modernists did relatively little theorizing about readers and reading. Happily, some others did it for them. The criticism which evolved out of the writer-reader disjunction that so bothered the Modernists led to a number of aesthetic theories, of which two are especially useful for understanding the early part of the *Collected Poems*. Over many years the American philosopher John Dewey (1859-1952) developed a theory designed to remove art from its pedestal, to remove it from its isolation in museums, and to re-place it firmly within the hustle and bustle of everyday life, both in the literal sense of feeling its presence (or absence) everywhere, and in the figurative sense of re-defining the value of Art in and to an industrial and increasingly egalitarian world. That theory was eventually published in book-form in 1935, under the title *Art as Experience*.

Dewey's idea that poetry was not words which had been put on a page for the reader's contemplation, but an experience on the part of a reader, set in motion by the words on the page, opened a way out of the universally perceived 'difficulty' of modern poetry. The poem itself could be seen pragmatically, as an experience, a reciprocal and interdependent exchange between writer and reader. In such a view, the 'difficulty' of reading poetry, as opposed to prose, would be amply rewarded by the unique value afforded by the poetic experience. As critic and educationalist Louise Rosenblatt (1904-2005) put it:

> Someone else can read the newspaper or a scientific work for us and summarize it acceptably. But no-one can read a poem for us.

The reader of the poem must have the experience himself. [ROSENBLATT, 1938, p. 33]

The Cambridge and Harvard critic I.A. Richards (1893-1979), whom Eliot admired while at the same time pretending that he did not understand him, drew on Dewey's ideas for his own *Principles of Literary Criticism* (1924) and applied them in *Practical Criticism* (1929). Subtitled *A Study in Literary Judgment*, the latter is an account of what happens when students read texts without knowing whom they have been written by. It is the first book-length example of close reading and its effects. The idea was not new of course, but a re-reading in a modern setting of what Alexander Pope had said so wittily some 200 years previously:

What woeful stuff this madrigal would be,
In some starv'd hackney sonneteer, or me?
But let a Lord once own the happy lines,
How the wit brightens! how the style refines!
Before his sacred name flies every fault,
And each exalted stanza teems with thought! [POPE, 1958, p. 68]

CLOSE READING

Close reading is an exercise to which every student of literature is trained nowadays. Students seldom find it difficult when, under the guise of Stylistics or Discourse Analysis, the close reading method is applied to prose, but they tend to find it less helpful in drawing out a meaning from poetry. And yet the purpose is the same: to go from an apparent meaning to a hidden one. And the same three-step method applies: first observe the linguistic components of the text, then select from these observations so as to order the evidence for an argument as to what the words mean, arranged as they are on the page, and then present that argument in plain critical prose.

The first step towards literary analysis consists of simple uninterpreted observations which, because poems are complex are best to carried out in five stages. First, observe, dispassionately, the **semiotic elements** of the poem: the blank spaces, capital letters, dropped lines, stanza layout, line lengths, punctuation and so on. Next, listen to the **sound effects**: accents, alliteration, anaphora, assonance, consonance, rhythm (in terms of metrics where useful, or simply cadence), rhyme, number of syllables... Then, note down the **syntax** of the poem: the use of pronouns and deictics, the frequency of certain parts of speech, link words, mood, types of sentences, use of tenses, use of the active or passive voice etc. Only fourthly, should we think about the **semantic** elements: the lexical field, word-associations, paradox, polysemy, the title... Finally, we should consider any outstanding **stylistic devices**: allegory, allusion, anaphora, antithesis, apostrophe, chiasmus, euphemism, hyperbole, irony, litotes, metaphor, metonymy, objective correlative, oxymoron, parallelism, personification, simile, zeugma... (see Glossary).

The listing of such observations might at first appear fastidious but after a little practice, this layered kind of reading comes more easily, and it is absolutely necessary if one wants really to experience the poem. With ordinary prose the syntax and semantics will usually suffice for our understanding, and for most rhetoric we need only recognize a few obvious stylistic devices, but in poetry the auditory and visual elements are essential to the rich and complex meaning. The whole point of poetry is to slow us down so that we feel and think about another's meaning. To understand, and be understood by, others we must first connect with them through the sensible organs that enable us to look and listen, to feel, as Eliot might have put it, someone else's intelligent sensibility.

It is important that the final presentation not be a mere word-salad of observations. The last stage is the **selection** of what appear to you as key elements, which you can then rearrange into a reasoned **argument** as to what the poem, for you, means. Some of your observations can be left out because they are only conventional. Others will seem to you surprising, and will emerge while you make your observations as, for you, the key elements. We should not be taken aback by the fact that a poem will yield a different meaning to different people. "Be not afeard," said Caliban to the shipwrecked sailors, "The isle is full of noises / sounds and sweet airs, that give delight, and hurt not." (*The Tempest*, III, 2).

Since analysis *and* comparison are the main tools of the critic, let us add to these suggestions for close reading by analysis, something on comparison. Critical comparison is, among other things, the sense of what the poet, consciously or unconsciously, is *not* saying. It is anything that is excluded from the poem, a key element or word that is excluded. The elephant or the mouse in the room. Let us take, for example, these lines:

> No! I am not Prince Hamlet nor was meant to be;
> Am an attendant lord, one that will do (7)

Expressed in prose, this becomes: No! I am not Prince Hamlet, nor was **I** meant to be him; **I** am an attendant lord, one that will do. The comparison between prose and poetry immediately draws our attention to the absence of a subject: in both the first and the second line 'I' is missing. Its absence is meaningful: the speaker has so little sense of his own self-worth that he cannot even bring himself to use the personal pronoun that refers to that self. Unlike Walt Whitman, Prufrock neither can nor wants to write a "Song of Myself". As an ironic* character, he belittles himself. Feeling small, he can hardly proclaim, "I am large, I contain multitudes." [WHITMAN, 1973, p. 88].

Comparison draws our attention to the poet's choices. Why such a word and not another? It has been said that by writing the first three lines of "The Love-Song of J. Alfred Prufrock", Eliot changed the whole course of modern poetry:

> Let us go then, you and I,
> When the evening is spread out against the sky
> Like a patient etherized upon a table; (3)

If we can agree that these lines are indeed stunning, then I would suggest that their originality —their *newness* as a Modernist would have put it— owes much to the choice of the word 'etherized'. What does that word mean, exactly, and does it summon up the same image in everyone's mind? We might as well ask if everyone sees the same colour when we say the word 'red'. Poetry draws our attention to the connotations compacted into a single word and so to the immense power latent in the instability of language. Perhaps that is why the cover of *The Waste Land* features in films such as *Apocalypse Now* and *Oppenheimer.* The responsibility of the poet —and, we have been arguing, the reader— for what happens once that power is released is another matter, which will be discussed in the "After Eliot" chapter.

WHY READ?

Returning to Virginia Woolf's description of her ideal reader, we find in it the kind of reading she imagines such a reader would give. The 'kind of a whole' that she envisages is a three-dimensional reading, encompassing:

– a portrait of a man

– a sketch of an age

– a theory of the art of writing

Notice the indefinite article: each reading will be singular and individual, provisional, to be communicated and added to by others. Notice too how the three dimensions move outwards, from the particular to the general, through the metaphor of artistry: our reading begins with a 'portrait', it goes on to become a 'sketch' and ends up saying something about 'art' in general. And that is precisely what we shall set out to do in the next three chapters.

CONTEXTS

PORTRAIT OF A POET

> And when I am formulated, sprawling on a pin,
> When I am pinned and wriggling on the wall,
> Then how should I begin
> To spit out all the butt-ends of my days and ways?
> And how should I presume? (5)

It might indeed seem presumptuous to look at the *Collected Poems* in a biographical light, especially if to Prufrock's protestations we place Eliot's own ideas concerning the poet's personal relationship to his work:

> What every poet starts from is his own emotions.... Shakespeare, too, was occupied with the struggle —which alone constitutes life for a poet— to transmute his personal and private agonies into something rich and strange, something universal and impersonal. [ELIOT, 1932, p. 117. My ellipsis]

And yet the "personal and private agonies" *will* creep in, as Eliot noted they did for Dante and Shakespeare, and the reader cannot but wonder where the intensity of emotion in a poem comes from. Biographers help, among other things, to set the poem in context but sometimes they also drown the essential, either in the bias of the dialectic they have set up in order to prevent the story being "just one damned thing after another", or else in an excess of detail. The story of Eliot's life has been told by several biographers so far, each from a different angle: Lyndall Gordon (twice), Carole Seymour-Smith, Robert Crawford (twice), James Miller... but I believe the first and shortest is still the best: Peter Ackroyd's *T.S. Eliot* (1984). It is on this biography that we shall draw in this chapter. With the recent release of all the known letters, in eight volumes, the problem of the overaccumulation of detail has only got worse, but the volumes of letters do have one striking advantage: each contains its own "Biographical commentary" which in a few pages gives an excellent overview of the context surrounding the writing of any given poem. When a single poem is under study, the 'commentary' in *The Poems of T.S. Eliot*, annotated by Jim McCue and Christopher Ricks, becomes invaluable.

Biographers of poets tend to follow the example of biographers in general in their desire to breathe new life into a once-living, breathing human being but, even if they somehow manage to unearth the "bundle of contradictions that sits down to breakfast" [Yeats, 1961, p. 1] his looming —or, in Eliot's case, lolling or stooping— presence tends to cast a shadow which stands between us and the poem. Knowledge of the man may be helpful to psychoanalytical critics because he can then quite legitimately be turned into a personality type, the study of whom will be their interpretation of the poem. But for the pragmatic, common reader, a biography serves a different purpose. The poem, not the poet, is our concern and the relationship between the two can be made by drawing a figurative parallel between the embodied, situated poet and the embodied, situated poem. The 'body' of a poem is made up of the words arranged on the page, and wafted on the air, essential elements which can be studied on their own, as we saw the students of I.A. Richards do. But is it best to do so? Can we not also situate the *poem*? Surely it is helpful to know something of the personal circumstances out of which it was written.

Awareness of the material, the phenomenal conditions out of which writing is born will enhance our critical reading. For example, in a letter to his Harvard friend Conrad Aiken in 1916 Eliot had this to say about his writing of prose reviews:

> Composing on the typewriter, I find that I am sloughing off all my long sentences which I used to dote upon. Short, staccato, like modern French prose. The typewriter makes for lucidity, but I am not sure that it encourages subtlety. [Eliot, 1988, p. 143]

Among the many elements which go to make up a poem, it is good to have information about where and when a particular poem was written, and out of what personal preoccupations which happened to be pressing upon the poet at the time. That is what we shall try to in this chapter: giving not a potted biography but just enough of the known facts about the life as will help us to *situate* the work, isolating the personal elements which nourish certain themes in the poetry. Ours will be a kind of post-impressionist* portrait, and we shall all the while bear in mind the sound literary principle that "What goes to the *making* of a poem does not necessarily go to its *meaning*." [RICKS, 2002, p. 157. My emphasis].

Let us presume to begin —for the purposes of clarity only—by dividing Eliot's life, from his birth in 1888 to his formal separation from his first wife in 1932, into five unequal periods. For each of these we shall evoke the main events of the life in order to see, if only briefly, how these fit into the main themes of the poetry.

1888-1910

During these years T.S. Eliot was born, grew up and was educated in the bustling industrial town of St. Louis, in what had previously been the Southern slave-state of Missouri. The atmosphere would have been something like that of Mark Twain's *Adventures of Huckleberry Finn*, a book which, having been forbidden to read as a boy, Eliot was only too pleased to preface in later life. Biographer Peter Ackroyd shrewdly draws on Theodor Dreiser's impressions of the city:

> Dreiser had come to St Louis as a journalist in the 1890s, and he described it as a rich and successful town, but one that had grown dormant in a kind of soft decay. The fog of "The Love Song of J. Alfred Prufrock" is the fog that blew from the factory chimneys across the Mississippi—drab, an exhalation of urban squalor. Children who live in such places grow up amid dereliction and rapid decay—and for those of a sensitive nature, the first awakening impressions are associated with images that spring from such decay. Throughout his life, Eliot was to derive a strange pleasure from walking through the alleys and the slums. [ACKROYD, 1988, p. 24]

The name "Prufrock" itself, Eliot later said, was a name he had seen on the side of a warehouse in St. Louis.

Eliot's parents were both in their forties when he was born. His father was nearly deaf, a successful businessman, and emotionally distant towards his children. His mother was a schoolteacher, fond of writing improving Victorian verse, and rather overprotective of her last child. Eliot had four sisters, the eldest of whom, Ada, was already nineteen when he was born, and a brother Henry, also deaf, who was nine. Eliot's mother's no doubt excessive solicitude towards him came from the fact that Tom was a child in frail health, often ill, and born with a double hernia which necessitated his wearing a truss until it could be (partially) cured by operation. It might also have been due to the fact that in the eight-year gap between Henry and Tom there had been a sixth child, Theodora, a 'gift of God' who had been taken away by death. Present, I think, in Eliot's work is the ghost of the little sister who had been loved and lost, and was not to be replaced by the troublesome Tom. It is there, most obviously, in the portrait of the artist as a young boy in "Animula" (103-4) but it is also in the obsessive connection between birth and death, in the Shakespearian theme of the lost child, of a gift taken away and another one unwanted. If, for instance, we take the line from "Prufrock" previously quoted, out of its immediate context, we may read it in quite a different way:

> No! I am not Prince Hamlet, nor was meant to be,

Spoken by Prufrock, these words are understood as "I was not meant to be Prince Hamlet"; they are humourously self-deprecating, lightly self-satirical. But if we listen to the poet's voice behind the mask of Prufrock, "nor was meant to be" will be understood as "nor was meant to be born", the forlorn cry of the child who feels unloved. Such is the force of poetry, "something almost being said". The seeming happiness of Eliot's well-to-do childhood masked the inner anguish of survivor's guilt. Christopher Ricks likes to connect Eliot with Bob Dylan; given the theme of the missing child, perhaps a deeper connection exists between Eliot and Elvis.

Perhaps his mother and his Irish nurse Annie, anxious that he should not wander and drown in the nearby Mississippi, filled his head with gruesome tales of drowned men? Certainly, he would hear of such when the river was in flood. Growing up beside a mighty river, Eliot later acknowledged, was an almost 'incommunicable' experience which gives force to the many rivers, streams, and springs that flow, or refuse to flow, through his poetry. We find both the incommunicable and the forceful in the line which opens the third part of *The Waste Land*: "The river's tent is broken..." (60). Like Langston Hughes, Eliot knew rivers and struggled to speak of them.

Eliot's feeling for water informs his poetry in ways perhaps best explored by Gaston Bachelard. To this was added a love for the sea, for sailing, and for those who go down to the sea in ships, which came from the long summers he spent on the Atlantic Ocean, in Maine and in the house built by his father in East Gloucester, Massachusetts. Long before "Marina" (105), sea and seashore images make unexpected appearances in Eliot's poems, often as images of the enigmatic other:

> And a crab one afternoon in a pool,
> An old crab with barnacles on his back,
> Gripped the end of a stick which I held him. (17)

Eliot's southern childhood came to an end when he was sent to Boston (first Milton Academy, then Harvard) for his studies. As an undergraduate, what most marked his poetry were his reading of *The Symbolist Movement in Literature* (1899, 1919) and a renewed acquaintance with the Bostonian branch of his family and their friends. In the introduction to Arthur Symons' ground-breaking study, Eliot, as he freely admitted, found his own poetic vocation:

> Here then, in this revolt against exteriority, against rhetoric, against a materialistic tradition; in this effort to disengage the ultimate essence, the soul, of whatever exists and can be realized by the consciousness; in this dutiful waiting upon every symbol by which the soul of things can be made visible, literature, bowed down by so many burdens, may at last attain liberty, and its authentic speech. [SYMONS, 1919, p. 9]

Not only is Symons' short introduction the indispensable guide to the poetry of Eliot's first two collections, and beyond, but so are his actual choice of French poets (Gérard de Nerval, Théophile Gautier, Charles Baudelaire, Villiers de l'Isle-Adam, Stéphane Mallarmé, Paul Verlaine, Arthur Rimbaud, Jules Laforgue), and his appeal to the force of symbolism equally present in prose as well as poetry.

After such heady reading, it was little surprise that the prosaic and appearance-seeking world of Boston became a mere irritant to Eliot, and one that he was to satirize so skillfully in his first two collections.

1911-1914

Inspired by the French Symbolists, and perhaps too by *Bubu de Montparnasse*, Charles-Louis Philippe's novel of poverty and prostitution (1901), T.S. Eliot persuaded his parents to pay for him to take a gap year in Paris, with digressions to Italy and Munich. (It was in Munich that he finished the writing of "Prufrock", storing it away until called upon to recite it at a gathering of E.R. Dodds' 'Coterie' at Merton College, Oxford). The Parisian experience was clearly momentous for Eliot, and it has been covered extensively by Nancy Duvall Hargrove in *T.S. Eliot's Parisian Year* (2009). Suffice it for us to note that it was during this year that he attended, with diminishing enthusiasm, the lectures of Henri Bergson, that he developed a lifelong admiration for Charles Maurras, and that he became close friends with Jean Verdenal, whose poetic career was to be cut short by his death in the Dardanelles. The only poem actually written during the year in Paris is "Rhapsody on a Windy Night", which is why it is vital to read that poem from that perspective. Elsewhere and otherwise, the contrast between this year of freedom and *bonhomie* and the return to Boston and Harvard for two years of postgraduate work was later to provide a second source of inspiration for Eliot's satirical gift.

His choice of philosophy as the main subject of his postgraduate course would also add new themes to the poetry. He studied under Irving Babbitt and George Santayana, but the elements that resurface most clearly in the poetry emanate from the elective courses on Eastern philosophy, on Buddhism particularly. Striking also was the visit of Bertrand Russell, whose incongruous presence in a Boston drawing-room is wittily satirized in "Mr. Apollinax". Bertrand Russell was for a time to become a mentor and friend of Eliot's, but his somewhat more-than-friendship with Eliot's wife led the poet to add, in 1915, some deliciously savage touches to his portrait of a philandering philosopher.

Russell was well-known for his Liberal, Free-thinking, and soon-to-be prominent pacifist principles. Eliot shared none of these views, but he was, albeit implicitly, in the poems, to engage with the reductive ideas about language that Russell, the Logical Atomists and the New Realists were debating at this time. He did this partly through the ideas that he had internalized from the Symbolists, and partly through the works that he chose as the subject of his PhD: F.H. Bradley's *Appearance and Reality* (1893, 1897) and *Essays on Truth and Reality* (1914).

A further source of inspiration from this time were the amateur theatricals in which he participated at his cousin Elinor Hinkley's house, and where in 1912 he met and fell in love with Emily Hale. That love story, which flourished intermittently until Eliot's surprise second marriage in 1958, can be read in his letters to her, only recently released, and free-to-access at the T.S. Eliot website. Lyndall Gordon's biography of *The Hyacinth Girl: T.S. Eliot's Hidden Muse* (2022) offers a much fuller account, including in a broader perspective all the women with whom Eliot was intimate. Alternatively, a close reading of "La Figlia Che Piange" might tell us, quite beautifully, all we need to know of what Eliot wanted from a woman.

1914-1918

Having obtained a fellowship to study for his doctorate at Bradley's own college of Merton, Oxford, Eliot sailed to Europe for a second time in late July, 1914. He went first to Marburg Germany, to attend a summer course which was cancelled by the outbreak of war, whereupon he made his way to London. That short stay no doubt shaped his even-handed view of the conflict since, as he put it, he saw "great moral earnestness on both sides". Although trapped in England for the duration of the war (and in fact well beyond), Eliot, as an American, was at first officially neutral. His status as a 'resident alien' is an oddly apt metaphor for his general attitude to his social surroundings. Although aware of the appalling conditions in the trenches, what he complained of most were the conditions that he himself endured in London and Oxford: poverty, boredom and censorship. The climate of England certainly did not agree with him: he was almost continually ill. Eliot, however, was inclined to think that ill-health might be propitious to the writing of certain kinds of poetry:

> I know, for instance, that some forms of ill-health, debility, or anaemia, may (if other circumstances are favourable) produce an efflux of poetry in a way approaching the condition of automatic writing —though, in contrast to the claims sometimes made for the latter, the material has obviously been incubating within the poet, and cannot be suspected of being a present from a friendly or impertinent demon. What one writes in this way may succeed in

> standing the examination of a more normal state of mind; it gives me the impression, as I have just said, of having undergone a long incubation, though we do not know until the shell breaks what kind of egg we have been sitting on. To me it seems that at these moments, which are characterized by the sudden lifting of the burden of anxiety and fear which presses upon our daily life so steadily that we are unaware of it, what happens is something negative: that is to say, not 'inspiration' as we commonly think of it, but the breaking down of strong habitual barriers — which tend to re-form very quickly. [ELIOT, 1933, p. 133]

This quotation explains, if nothing else, the title of "A Cooking Egg". The general atmosphere of drabness, war-weariness, and poverty explains also the subject-matter of all the poems written during this time, which have a minor-key or light-verse quality, and seek their inspiration in memories of France and Boston. The poems written in French, the brief satirical sketches of his inner and outer life in Boston, the quatrain and Sweeney poems: all these hark back to happier times.

Eliot's spur-of-the-moment marriage to Vivien Haigh-Wood in June 1915, which he later attributed to war circumstances, seems to have been a disaster almost from the start. Biographers have done much to rescue Vivien's reputation, but they cannot rescue the marriage. As Tom put it many years later, "To her the marriage brought no happiness... to me it brought the state of mind out of which came *The Waste Land*."

1919-1925

That 'state of mind' in fact brought into being three of Eliot's major poems: "Gerontion", *The Waste Land*, and "The Hollow Men". Eliot's "rhythmic grumbling" in these three poems echoes the chaos of the aftermath of war, encapsulating in a few lines the 'world crisis' which it took Winston Churchill six volumes (1923-31) to describe. This conjunction of the private and the public is, for many of his older contemporary readers, what makes Eliot's poetry so distinctive. His younger readers, those who were to be called 'the Brideshead generation' heard *The Waste Land* differently. Like Anthony Blanche in Waugh's novel, they would recite the poem for the sheer joy of its stately mock-solemnity:

> After luncheon he stood on the balcony with a megaphone which had appeared surprisingly among the bric-à-brac of Sebastian's room, and in languishing sobbing tones recited passages from The Waste land to the sweatered and muffled throng that was on its way to the river.
> "I, Tiresias, have foresuffered all," he sobbed to them from the Venetian arches:
> Enacted all on this same d-divan or b-bed,
> I who have sat by Thebes below the wall
> And walked among the lowest of the dead...
> And then, stepping lightly into the room, "How I have surprised them!" [WAUGH, 1945, p. 30-31]

It was during this period that Eliot wrote the 'Unfinished Poems' of our selection. Why could he not finish them? Was it because the form of dramatic poetry, in all its variations, was no longer fit for purpose and a new form, the verse drama, was needed?

1926-1932

Eliot later saw 1926 as a turning-point in his life. It was in this year that he gave up his job at Lloyds Bank, and took up the post at the publishing house of Faber & Gwyer (later Faber & Faber) that was to last until his death in 1965. The *Criterion* was relaunched from Faber's, as *The New Criterion* (of course). Eliot's very own 'little magazine' carried over the same principle from the old to the new:

> It is the function of a literary review to maintain the autonomy and disinterestedness of literature, and at the same time to exhibit the relations of literature — not to 'life', as something contrasted to literature, but to all the other activities, which, together with literature, are the components of life. (*The Criterion*, 1923, p. 421)

In 1926 Eliot's poems also took up their permanent home at Faber's: in *Poems 1909-1925*, the first two collections, *The Waste Land* and "The Hollow Men" were published together, in what was to be the first of the three *Collected Poems* (1926, 1936, 1963).

Crucially, 1926 was the year when Eliot —after much private reading of Christian texts such as those of St. Thomas Aquinas, St. John of the Cross, and, in a modern perspective, Jacques Maritain, and after a rather public display of falling to his knees in front of Michelangelo's *Pietà* in Rome— was secretly received into the Church of England. His conversion was announced in 1927, to accompany his taking up of British citizenship and the publication of his Clark lectures at Cambridge, under the title of *For Lancelot Andrewes*. In the preface to that book, Eliot made the self-proclamation that he had become a "Classicist in taste, Royalist in politics, and Anglo-Catholic in religion". Perhaps he had always been, secretly, so?

As such things often do, Eliot's conversion dismayed his readers. Perhaps it also made them, as it should do us, reread his work up to that time for the premises of a religious faith. These lines in *The Waste Land*, for example, seem to presage his conversion, as they certainly suggest an association between Church and beauty:

> Where fishmen lounge at noon: where the walls
> Of Magnus Martyr hold
> Inexplicable splendour of Ionian white and gold. (62-63)

It is at this point that we remember that Eliot was born into the Unitarian faith of his Bostonian family. Unitarianism is a far cry from High Anglicanism, as Peter Ackroyd explains:

> Unitarianism is, in fact, from the perspective of orthodoxy, an heretical faith principally because it does not accept the Christian doctrine of the Incarnation — Christ becoming a sort of superior Emerson. It is essentially Puritanism drained of its theology, since it denies the central tenets of predestination and damnation; heaven and hell are of less account than the mundane space we inhabit between them. The measure of Man is Man himself and a peculiarly American optimism, about the progress and perfectibility of humankind, is thereby given a quasi-spiritual sanction. Unitarianism is earnest, intellectual, humanitarian, part of that high-minded 'ethical culture' which Eliot in later years distrusted and mocked. [ACKROYD, 1988, p. 17]

This throws as much light on "Whispers of Immortality" (45) and "Mr. Eliot's Sunday Morning Service" (47) as it does on "Ash Wednesday" (85-95) and the Ariel poems (99-106). The accent in Eliot's Anglo-Catholicism is on 'Catholic'. In his interest in the late Elizabethan dramatists, he was clearly drawn to the time of the Counter-Reformation and its Mannerist art. The image of a divine and suffering Christ ubiquitous in Roman Catholicism but absent from the faith of his fathers, was crucial to Eliot's religious *feeling*. It is telling that the image he brought back from his first trip to France was Paul Gauguin's *Yellow Christ:* perhaps because, as Ackroyd speculates, "the artist painted his own features on the sallow and shrunken body on the Cross;" [ACKROYD, 1988, p. 52]

Ackroyd also has something, doubtlessly more debatable, to say about the effect of Eliot's conversion on the poems which enact it:

> In poetry, belief need play no part; and within Eliot's own work, the structure of orthodox faith and the language of devotion are broken apart, in order to make room for something much stranger and more tenuous, like the sound of someone crying in an empty church. [ACKROYD, 1988, p. 163]

We need not agree with Ackroyd's simile* to feel that there is indeed something 'strange and tenuous' in the religious poems, and it is perhaps this which makes them beautiful.

One thing is for sure: the last period of our selection closes with Eliot's formal separation from his first wife. That break —with the deep sense of fear and guilt that was to follow— is figured on the very cover of *Ash Wednesday*, where 'Wednesday' graphically returns to its original meaning of weddings-day, a day which, for Eliot, had turned into sackcloth and ashes:

ASH
WEDNES
DAY

A SKETCH OF AN AGE

> It is impossible to read the compositions of the most celebrated writers of the present day without being startled with the electric life which burns within their words. They measure the circumference and sound the depths of human nature with a comprehensive and all-penetrating spirit, and they are themselves perhaps the most sincerely astonished at its manifestations; for it is less their spirit than the spirit of the age.
>
> —Percy Bysshe Shelley, "A Defence of Poetry", 1821

Like the relationship between the man and his art, the connection between the artist and his age is a natural but complex one, and for that reason we shall give here, as Virginia Woolf advises, not the finished painting but only the roughest of sketches. And for the sake of clarity, once again, we shall reduce what were in the last chapter seen as five periods in Eliot's life up to 1932, to the three most productive periods, as seen in the *Collected Poems* (1963):

- the 23 poems written between 1909 and 1918
- "Gerontion", *The Waste Land*, and "The Hollow Men" 1919-1925
- *Ash-Wednesday* and the Ariel poems 1926-1930

We will look at each group in turn from the point of view of one aspect of the larger culture that was seen at the time as 'modern' (see "Cousin Nancy", 22) and that we now call Modernist. Only one aspect of Modernism has been developed in relation to each group, but it goes (almost) without saying that the aspects can be applied retrospectively or prospectively to the other groups, and that there are of course many other aspects of the multifaceted Modernist movement in Eliot's poetry that we might have developed.

Running through our argument, more or less explicitly, will be a theme that might be considered appropriate to all of Eliot's poetry, and that is the theme of **clairvoyance**. It was suggested to me by Peter Ackroyd who, in the biography to which we alluded in the last chapter, made this perspicacious remark about Eliot:

> He had, I believe, a clairvoyant sense of his time — clairvoyant because he found its preoccupations within himself. [ACKROYD, 1988, p. 107]

This remark rings true, but for our purposes it will need some clarification and a few caveats. The *Oxford English Reference Dictionary* (1992) definition of 'clairvoyance' is quite simple, but it carries three shades of meaning which we can set out thus:

> **clairvoyance**: **1.** The supposed faculty of perceiving things or events in the future, or **2.** beyond normal sensory contact **3**. exceptional insight.

If Eliot was clairvoyant, it was in the second and third senses of the term, rather than the first. *Quoique*... the idea casts new light on the speaker's vision at the end of "Portrait of a Lady":

> Well! and what if she should die some afternoon,
> Afternoon grey and smoky, evening yellow and rose;
> Should die and leave me sitting pen in hand
> With the smoke coming down above the housetops;
> Doubtful, for a while
> Not knowing what to feel or if I understand
> Or whether wise or foolish, tardy or too soon...
> (12. Eliot's ellipsis)

It casts new light too on the Madame Sosostris episode in *The Waste Land* (54). The predominant tone is satirical, towards an age which, having lost its Christian faith, was more than usually interested in the supernatural and readily turned to charlatans. Eliot himself once visited a fortune-teller, before leaving the United States for Europe in 1914 [ELIOT, 1988, p. 37] and, like W.B. Yeats though less profoundly, he was interested in the occult. But, beyond these cultural considerations, can we not read the passage as textually clairvoyant, a kind of dramatic irony*, the seven Tarot cards announcing symbolic figures to come? This in addition to the function of the passage as an allegory of reading (what we see and do not see, our attitude to what puzzles us) and indeed of Art (in Platonic terms, a copy of a copy of the True).

To return to our definition, it becomes even more pertinent to Eliot's poetry if we consider clairvoyance as an unusual perception of the present and the *past*, and the relationship between the two (see A close reading…, and Allusion). For the clairvoyant, the past is a haunting presence. All artists, we will agree, have 'exceptional insight' but the generation which had read Bradley's *Appearance and Reality* —and none more keenly than Eliot— was also highly conscious of the difference between what we think we see and what we are not sure we feel, between the outer and inner worlds in which we live and move and have our being. Nor was it a question of one sense only: Eliot, as we can tell from the poems, was highly sensitive to sounds, to touch, to taste and to smells. His remembering "a slice of lemon, and a bitten macaroon" (23) was, in miniature and in its own way, a Proustian moment.

With these points, and more, in mind, let us turn to our groups of poems and the cultural perspectives which might help us to read them. Bearing in mind that one of the examinations which make up the *agrégation* is the *épreuve hors programme*, our perspective on the poetry will be resolutely intermedial*.

THE BOSTONIAN POEMS: FRAMING THE MOMENT

With only two exceptions ("Rhapsody on a Windy Night" which is connected to Paris, and "Gerontion" which I have placed in the second group) all the poems in *Prufrock and Other Observations* and *Poems* (3-50) were written in the nine years between 1909 and 1918, and they were all written in or about Boston. Like the stories in *Dubliners*, many of these poems dramatize a slowly dying age, the older *fin-de-siècle* generation bewildered by an increasingly intrusive and rebellious new one. It is the world of Henry Adams, whose autobiography was reviewed favourably by Eliot when it was published posthumously in 1918. Written in the third person, self-distancing, Adams' autobiography builds up to a dramatic climax, in which the elderly statesman stands in Chartres cathedral and meditates on the contrast between the stable world of the thirteenth century, symbolized in a statue of the Virgin, and the constantly accelerating world of the modern age, symbolized in the mechanics of the Dynamo. To this temporal contrast between past and present, the fine irony* and the transatlantic theme of Eliot's poems add a spatial dimension which owes much to Henry James (1843-1916); not just *Portrait of a Lady* (1881) but James' short stories, a novel such as *The Bostonians* (1886) or the travel-essay which is *The American Scene* (1907) haunt Eliot's drawing-rooms.

So much of the old world dying, but what of the new one struggling to be born? It is precisely this moment that is *dramatized* in Eliot's Bostonian poems: a single moment for the shorter poems, a series of moments for the longer ones. The verb might seem to indicate that it would be useful to read the poems in terms of the theatre, and this is so, but it might also be helpful to read them in relation to fine art. The theatrical moment could then be likened to the pause at the end of an act, before the curtain falls, when the actors freeze on stage and the audience is invited to *contemplate* the scene. The drama of Eliot's poems comes at just such a freeze-frame moment, the speaker hesitating on a staircase for example or poised pen in hand, as in our above example. This is Eliot's particular connection to Imagism*: not the simple fact that he frequented the Imagists and was published in *Blast*, but his presentation of life in terms of arresting images, or *tableaux vivants*. Pound's haiku-like poem "In a station of the Metro" is often presented as the archetype of the Imagist poem: it too is a *tableau vivant*.

Freeze-framing, as its name implies, is a term borrowed from what was in Eliot's time the newly-invented art of cinematography, an art form with which he does not seem to have had much sympathy. Since old art forms tend to develop in reaction to a newly-invented one, we might briefly consider Eliot's poetry and some of the art of his time in terms of such a reaction. Cinematography is fundamentally the art of the *moving* picture: in its early days, a rapid, flickering succession of images and a world depicted as frenetic action, an art more on the side of the Dynamo than of the Virgin. Some fine art of the time reflected the anxiety induced by such incessant movement (or 'acceleration', as Henry Adams called it): for example, Marcel Duchamp's second painting (1912) of a *Nude Descending a Staircase*. (For these and other art references, see Webliography). Eliot's speaker's moments of doubt and hesitancy are not necessarily reprehensible paralysis; they can also be salutary moments of contemplation, of being still. Secondly, film was silent until 1927; both inner monologue and dialogue were very clumsily conveyed by histrionic expressions and poorly-written slides. Eliot's dramatic monologues and his use of polyphonic voices are witty proof of what poetry can do and, at the time, film could not. Besides which, the silences in the poems are in pleasant contrast to the cacophonous piano which accompanied the silent film. Finally, films, like photographs, were commonly in black-and-white: hence (in part) the enthusiasm for colour in the portraiture of, say, John Singer Sergeant or the Fauvist landscapes.

Eliot was interested in painting and even before settling in Europe he was a regular visitor to the Boston house of Isabella Stewart-Gardner, whose fine collection was even then (in)famous for its incongruous mixture of dour family portraits and flamboyant modern art. Eliot's poems clearly have affinities with well-known Modernist painters —every reader will find their preferred pairing for a given poem— and Wyndham Lewis's 1938 portrait of Eliot is a kind of poem in itself but, in this brief sketch, and for theoretical purposes, it might be helpful to mention two less well-known examples.

The first is a British painter currently coming back into fashion: Walter Sickert (1860-1942). Having studied in France under Degas, the unfortunately named Sickert had a considerable influence on British painting for the first three decades of the twentieth century. His painting has a dark side which is somewhat in keeping with the moody side of Eliot. Like Eliot, he had a fascination for the seedy side of city life, including sensational murders: the world, in fact of 'Sweeney'. His early theatre paintings are a good illustration of the 'gallery fright' which Eliot imputed to contemporary readers. The striking series of 'Conversation Pieces' —*Ennui* (1914) in particular— are framed fragments of a story that is suggested rather than told, and are a silent version of the snatches of conversation in Eliot's poems. Finally, we can connect, I think, Eliot's inner anguish to the scenes Sickert painted, of framed windows opening inwards onto drab, self-enclosed and frightening worlds.

Sickert attended both of the Post-Impressionist exhibitions held in London in 1911 and 1912. The justification required by the scandal provoked by the French painters exhibited by Roger Fry is interesting in that it was made in terms that are equally pertinent to Eliot's poetry. Sickert, for example, admired the abrupt yet delicate transitions within the paintings. Cézanne in particular was held up for admiration on account of his orderly compositions, the broken brushwork technique he used to create geometrical forms, the fragmented but harmonious blocks of colour, the everyday objects set on tilted table-tops, and the multiple perspectives proposed within a single painting. Any or all of these artistic qualities could just as well be used to describe, metaphorically, modern poetry.

"GERONTION", *THE WASTE LAND*, "THE HOLLOW MEN": THREE POEMS IN A MAJOR KEY

The poems written between 1919 and 1925 seem different in kind from the previous work: the tone more somber and disjointed. "What ails *The Waste Land*?" Alice Oswald asked in a recent Oxford poetry lecture. What ailed postwar Europe was what ailed Eliot: exhaustion, grief, disgust. These poems could of course be linked to the artistic expression of these emotions —all three could be comments on Paul Nash's *The Menin Road* (1919) for example— but given Eliot's exceptional ability to orchestrate voices and to distinguish music from discordant sound, we might do well to consider the poems in relation to some of the musical works of his time.

Once again, every reader will make her own connections to a particular piece of music. There are plenty of references to choose from: from music-hall and ragtime (57) to popular song. It might be the *Preludes* by Frédéric Chopin (8-9) or the incorporation of Richard Wagner's "Song of the Rhine Maidens" into part three of *The Waste Land* (63). At Igor Stravinsky's *Rite of Spring* which was revived by the Ballets Russes in 1920, Eliot is reported to have, uncharacteristically, stood up and cheered at the end. Eliot once said that he would like to transpose into poetry the "non-human gaiety which emerged from the other side of suffering" which he heard in Beethoven's A Minor Quartet, and *Four Quartets* has naturally been read from that perspective.

No doubt the same could be done from the more various musical notes in the early poems: "Under the juniper tree the bones sang, scattered and shining." (88). And, as with art exhibitions, the public reception of the work is as interesting as what can be gleaned of the performances themselves. The works need not be explicitly referenced in the poems: *succès de scandale* such as Erik Satie's *Parade* (1917) or William Walton's musical accompaniment to Edith Sitwell's *Façade*, are part of the Modernist musical background, as is the kind of listening they affront, or solicit.

My own preference, if I may briefly be allowed to have one, would go to the connections —or, rather the extraordinary absence of connections— between T.S. Eliot and Ralph Vaughan Williams (1872-1958). The "Fantasia on a Theme by Thomas Tallis" caused a sensation when it was first performed in Gloucester Cathedral in 1910, and the ways in which the sixteenth-century melody is incorporated into the modern work strike me as having real affinities with the Eliot's compositional method. Vaughan William's setting, in 1914, of George Meredith's poem "The Lark Ascending" is considered to be the finest short work by an English composer in the twentieth century. How could such an Anglophile and *mélomane* as Eliot have simply passed it by? And what to make of his silence on Vaughan William's *Pastoral Symphony*, which premiered in 1922? The 'pastoral' refers to a painting by Corot and the fields of the fallen in France, the real waste land. Were we to ask him about this, perhaps Eliot would return the same answer as W.H. Auden who once ruefully admitted, "Occasionally I come across a book which I feel has been written for me and for me only. Like a jealous lover, I don't want anybody else to hear of it." [AUDEN, 1963, p. 13]

The key text underpinning any examination of the connections between what Eliot heard and what he was able to transmute into a poem of that experience is of course his critical reference to what he called 'the auditory imagination':

> What I call the 'auditory imagination' is the feeling for syllable and rhythm, penetrating far below the conscious levels of thought and feeling, invigorating every word; sinking to the most primitive and forgotten, returning to the origin and bringing something back, seeking the beginning and the end; it works through meanings, certainly, or not without meanings in the ordinary sense, and fuses the old and the obliterated and the trite,

the current and the new and the surprising, the most ancient and the most civilized mentality. [ELIOT, 1933, p. 118–119]

Feeling and fusion: how are these achieved in words? The answer to that will raise, at the very least, questions of cadence*, echo*, metre*, rhythm*, *motif**, onomatopoeia*, rhyme*, tone* and voice*; and how these work by harmony or counterpoint. In a word, how is a poem *orchestrated*?

ASH WEDNESDAY AND THE ARIEL POEMS: A RETURN TO RITUAL

In the attitude of, and the forms of address* and the use of anaphora* by the speaker in *Ash Wednesday*, and the fact that the Ariel poems were designed as gifts to be given at Christmas, we see Eliot return to the question of ritual*. Perhaps he did so in part to avoid what he saw as a dangerous tendency in modern criticism, running from Matthew Arnold to F.R. Leavis, by way of the Abbé Brémond, to find in poetry a source of religious or moral principles. The Modernist tendency, on the contrary, was to urge the irresponsibility of the poet and the disinterestedness of poetry.

Indeed, it was part of the strategy of a whole generation to focus on the question of ritual, either to mock the old or to invent the new. It was this quality that Eliot so admired in James Joyce, his ability to connect the primitive, ancient world of myth and ritual with the daily actions and habits of the modern world. Thus, the ekphrastic passage which opens "A Game of Chess" (56) evokes the ritual of a woman preparing to go out, contrasting the ancient and modern versions of that ritual act.

Eliot's generation had been made conscious of the power of ritual by the group known as the Cambridge Ritualists, who saw in Greek theatre traces of ancient rites. Their work was influenced and amplified by the flourishing new sciences of archeology and anthropology. Besides which, seeing social habits through the lens of ritual was a way of linking (evolutionary) nature and culture, since animals were also observed to perform mating and house-building rituals. So even Sweeney could be included in the ritual gaze.

Consciousness of ritual involves the kind of detached observation evidenced in the very title of *Prufrock and Other Observations*. In fact, Eliot had always been interested in ritual, and the early poems are rife with social rituals: tea-time, church-going, brothel visits, art exhibitions, eating out… "A penny for the old guy", the epigraph to "The Hollow Men" is a signpost to the annual commemoration of Guy Fawkes' Day. And is there not ritual in that marvelous image of "Hakagama, bowing among the Titians"? After the secret rituals of his reception into the Anglican Church, Eliot's sense of ritual became more acute but perhaps also more private and less easily communicated in poetry.

The end is where we start from (208)… In conclusion, let us return to the question of clairvoyance and its connection with predicting the future. The Modernist texts —the art, the literature, the music and other media we have not talked of here— that have survived into our own time, becoming 'modern classics', have done so because they had a certain amount of clairvoyance —seeing beyond normal sensory contact or possessed of exceptional insight— that enabled them to see more than the rest of their generation. But did that mean they could see into the future? Could they even, like Orestes, see the nemesis that awaited them, which the less mythically minded John Maynard Keynes called "the economic consequences of the Peace"? It would seem not. In a review of Eliot's *For Lancelot Andrewes*, Liberal critic Edmund Wilson complained, within months of the Wall Street Crash, that he found Eliot's seventeenth-century churchmen no more convincing than Dos Passos' army of workers. The Conservative (or worse) mind of the Anglo-American Modernists made them wish to reconstruct stable societies that had never in fact existed:

> Only in a closely-knit and homogeneous society, where many men are at work on the same problems, such a society as those which produced the Greek chorus, the Elizabethan lyric, and the Troubadour canzone, will the development of such [modern] forms ever be carried to perfection. [ELIOT, 1965, p. 189]

Therein lay the rub: too great a fear of the diverse and disorderly tends toward the intolerant and the totalitarian.

TOWARDS A THEORY OF...

Boswell: "Then, Sir, what is poetry?"
Johnson: "Why, Sir, it is much easier to say what it is not.
We all *know* what light is; but it is not easy to *tell* what it is."
—Boswell, *Life of Johnson* (1791)

A 'theory of the art of writing', we recall, was the third and last component of the "some kind of whole" that common readers would construct out of their reading. After 'a portrait of a poet' and 'a sketch of an age' and continuing our natural movement from the particular to the general, we must now consider the work of theorizing, not for its own sake, but in order to construct 'some kind of whole'.

We shall retain the perspective we have employed so far, focussed on the reader, but we can now extend it to the wider view of the reception of poetry in the modern era. The poet, the writer, has a finite writing life: in Eliot's case, let us say from 1909-1945 or, as far as we are concerned, from 1909-1930. Naturally, we can expect and detect a certain evolution in the poet's style between those dates, but it is a chronologically limited one. Once the poem is published it may undergo some changes, especially when being moved from magazine into book form but (with a few exceptions which hardly concern Eliot) it then becomes fixed on the page. In other words, what we may call the writing life of a poem is quite limited. The same is not true, on the other hand, of its reading life. That not only changes *with* every new generation of reader but also varies *among* readers of each generation. *One man's meat is another man's poison*, and new contexts produce new readers. Thus, there are no limits to what we might call the reading life of a published poem, or group of poems.

Given the sheer force of the numbers involved, it is very curious that so little attention has been paid to the readers of poetry. Those who in 1936 had received poetry "in a hostile spirit" gave way in 1951 to those who received it, according to Anne Ridler in a second edition of the *Faber Book Of Modern Verse*, with "indifference". Does it matter? Eliot, for one, thought so. He was acutely aware of the changing demands which different Ages (as he called them) made upon its poets. What he calls the 'historical sense' needed to draw up a history of the demands made upon poetry by its audience, makes up the entire theme of his Harvard lectures [ELIOT, 1933]. When he comes to summing up that theme, however, he stumbles upon a paradox:

> No two readers, perhaps, will go to poetry with quite the same demands. Amongst all these demands from poetry and responses to it there is always some permanent element in common, just as there are standards of good and bad writing independent of whatever any of us happens to like and dislike; but every element to formulate the common element is limited by the limitations of particular men in particular places and at particular times; and these limitations become manifest in the perspective of history. [ELIOT, 1933, p. 141]

Is it just the classicist in Eliot that believes there is "some permanent element in common" to all poetry, regardless of the historical demands made upon it, or can it be universally agreed that there is something in poetry that is a timeless force, a metaphysical element in the Aristotelian sense of 'unchanging'? If so, then can it be defined? Is it worth trying to define? The questions are genuinely open, not rhetorical, ones.

Characteristically, Eliot had in fact, at the beginning of his lecture course, gone some way to answering the questions he went on to imply at the end. He had begun by defining 'literary criticism', which in 1933 was still quite a new field of study, since the first Chair of English at Oxford University had only been created in 1900. Significantly, his definition involves stressing the interdependence of the two critical approaches to poetry which, nearly a century later, we instantly recognize: theory (*dissertation*) and close reading (*explication*):

> But there are these two theoretical limits of criticism: at one of which we attempt to answer the question 'what is poetry?' and at

> the other 'is this a good poem?'. No theoretic ingenuity will suffice to answer the second question, because no theory can amount to much which is not founded upon a direct experience of good poetry; but on the other hand, our direct experience of poetry involves a good deal of generalizing activity. [ELIOT, 1933, p. 16]

Today, we would have no problem agreeing that any theory of poetry must be based on direct experience of poems and that our direct experience involves "a good deal of generalizing activity". There would, I suspect, be less agreement as to what we mean by 'good' poetry. Even Eliot, after all, used the word 'good' in two different senses within the same sentence!

In fact, it is the question of literary criticism itself, which is problematic, and has been so from its turn-of-the-twentieth-century beginnings. To understand the impact that *lit. crit.* has had on the art of reading poetry, any poetry at all, we need to turn to a work which Eliot had to hand at the time of his own lecture course. In 1932 the poet and university teacher Lascelles Abercrombie (1881-1938) published *Principles of Literary Criticism*, in which he set out what distinguished literary criticism from other literary activities. What he had to say will be broken up into two distinct propositions which I would like to discuss, and, for present purposes, I will assume that what he says about 'literature' applies to poetry. He begins by saying:

> The power to enjoy literature is also quite different from the power to analyze it rationally. The power to enjoy literature, like the power to compose it, proceeds from a certain nature. Very probably, indeed, both powers proceed from the same nature; only in one case it exists passively, in the other actively. And now to these must be added a third power — the power to criticize literature. [ABERCROMBIE, 1932, p. 9]

Cast into our terms, there have always between those who write and those who 'enjoy' poetry: indeed, they are two sides of the same coin, the active poet and the passive reader. The literary critic differs from them in being able to analyze poetry rationally. He goes on to clarify this new-found analytic power:

> We may say, then, that the realm of literature is occupied by the activities of three distinct powers: the power to create, the power to enjoy, and the power to criticize. The chief thing that distinguishes the power to criticize from the other two is the fact that it can be acquired. For, though criticism may be intuitive, the critic may also be conscious of the process by which he criticizes; and this process appeals to certain intellectual principles which can be set out in an orderly system, studied and deliberately put into practice. [*Ibid.*, p. 9–10]

This passage is rather more self-serving than it might appear: for if the critical power, unlike the other two, can be acquired, then it can also be *taught*. And taught it has been, in the many English literature departments which have flourished since Abercrombie's time. Actually, since his time, so has (up to a point) "the power to create", in 'creative writing' classes. Only 'the power to 'enjoy' poetry has atrophied, both within the university and without, and this is perhaps the 'dissociation of sensibility' which characterizes our own time. The remedy is to once again bring together the common reader who 'enjoys' poetry, and the critical reader who analyses it. If Eliot did not find the two types of reading antagonistic [ELIOT, 1933, p. 36] then neither need we.

In their haste to turn literary criticism into a science, set apart from common or garden reading because it is based on rational analysis, critics have tended to reduce poetry to what G.M. Hopkins called 'the teachable element': in a word, the study of rhetoric. But, as C. Ricks pointed out, poetry offers something more than rhetoric, something which, history shows, it is unwise to leave out:

> Rhetoric, this teachable element in literature, is not theory, and it still has its legitimate claims and must not be ousted. Rhetoric, granted, is not literature, but that is not because the teachable element departs, rather because something else arrives, a ministering to wisdom, or to justice, or to vitality, or to magnanimity, such as does not need to rest content with persuasion. [RICKS, 1996, p. 312]

It is this 'something more', variable with each poem, which revitalizes our lives and makes reading poetry (and other genres) worthwhile. In order to recover it, we will have to abandon our pretentions to science, and return to the *art* of reading. "The power to enjoy literature, like the power to compose it, proceeds from a certain nature," said Abercrombie. Indeed so, but this is a universal power of *human* nature, and the powers of composition and enjoyment are *reciprocal* powers.

Pursuing the idea previously postulated, that poetry is "something almost being said", we can now reaffirm that the meaning of a poem is *co-constructed* by the poet and (in this case) his reader. And if we continue to think of art as experience, then it is an experience shared *between* poet and reader. In truth, their experiences mirror each other in a reciprocal act of giving and receiving. It is a mutual exchange in that not only does the reader assume the presence of a poet behind a persona, but the poet has already included his idea of the reader in the poem. As John Dewey put it, "To be truly artistic, a work must also be esthetic —that is, framed for enjoyed receptive production." [DEWEY, 1934, p. 48]. In fact, Dewey goes further than that, maintaining that any judgement that we make on a work of art must take into account the reciprocity of the exchange. "Perfection in execution," says Dewey, "cannot be measured or defined in terms of execution only; it implies those who perceive and enjoy the product that is executed." [DEWEY, 1934, p. 47].

This was true *before* the arrival of modern poetry. When poems were mostly sung, or recited, or in some way performed, audience participation was part of the poem. When verse followed predictable patterns of rhythm and rhyme, the auditors quite literally joined in by interjecting improvised but symmetrical stanzas of their own. Since this cannot happen when the poem becomes fixed on the page, nor is it possible with the free verse —free in the sense of unpredictable— of modern poetry, the reader has to find a new role to play. In making modern verse more 'difficult' the poet helps to provide the reader with that role, which is to read the poem as patiently and meticulously as the poet wrote it, so that once again, but in a new way, its meaning can be co-constructed.

So, the reader of modern poetry must be one who can both enjoy *and* criticize the poem. Since no two reading experiences draw on precisely the same sources, she may need the help of notes from time to time, and other reader's scholarship and insights will not be unwelcome, but she will follow, at least at the outset, her own inclinations, as Eliot himself, who distrusted the idea of 'taste', recommended. And it is largely for this reason, the demands that it makes on the reader, that *The Waste Land* is considered to be the archetype of Modernist poetry. Because of its highly allusive nature and elliptical structure, the poem depends for its very life on the reader providing the coherence that the poet has deliberately omitted. Naturally, a plurality of readers will interpret the poem in a plurality of ways. According to Peter Ackroyd:

> *The Waste Land* provided a scaffold on which others might erect their own theories; so that it has been variously interpreted as personal autobiography, an account of a collapsing society, an allegory of the Grail and spiritual rebirth, a Buddhist meditation. [ACKROYD, 1988, p. 120]

The list is by no means exhaustive, with every new generation of readers, and of readers within those generations, providing fresh insights. Indeed, the sheer wealth of literary criticism generated by Eliot's work is so great that it is at times dispiriting, and that is why, in view of the limited time available to *agrégatifs*, not to mention other common readers, I have refrained from exploiting it. We can safely leave that to others, while we, the common readers, equipped only with the expectation of pleasure and with only a minimum of help from B.C. Southam's guide or (better) C. Ricks' commentary, our time will be better spent silently listening for the poem, letting it come as softly to us as it once came to the poet:

> It comes blundering over the
> Boulders at night, it stays
> Frightened outside the
> Range of my campfire
> I go to meet it at the
> Edge of the light.
> (Gary Snyder, "How Poetry Comes to Me", 1992)

If art is experience and nobody else can have that experience for us, then we had better spend as much of our time as possible on determining exactly what and how much we *feel* for any given poem, or group of poems. We cannot of course do that until we have let the poem "do its work" on us, using the reading strategies outlined in the Introduction. But after that, as long as we keep our eyes on the poem —a wild and unpredictable creature, which has a habit of fleeing from us—

we are free to follow what paths we please into and out of, and alongside, the poem. Each reader will choose the guides he finds most congenial, pausing perhaps from time to time to pick out from the hundreds of definitions of poetry, the one best suited to structuring our thought-feelings about the poem(s) under study.

In addition to the definitions that can be found scattered throughout this study already, we might mention two others which might be found apposite to the "generalizing activity" which naturally follows on from the reading of a particular poem. Rather than discuss them at length, I shall put the kind of thinking that this involves in the form of numbered questions. The answers to the questions, which I leave to my readers to give, correspond to the three-part plan of a classic *dissertation*.

To what extent could Eliot's own definition of poetry as a 'superior amusement' [ELIOT, 1920, p. 9] structure our thought about one of his poems, or the selection of poems generally? Although he was quick to add that he did not mean 'an amusement for superior people', I am not sure that we should necessarily take that at face value: Eliot's need for 'order' had both a social and a cultural side. 1) The remark was made in 1920, and may apply differently to the poems written before that date, and those written afterwards. Eliot's perception of 'superiority' is very different, surely, in "Portrait of a Lady" from that which he suggests in *Ash-Wednesday*. 2) And what are the apparently demeaning implications of the term 'amusement'? 3) Perhaps the terms of his definition are meant to balance each other out?

We might prefer to structure an argument by agreeing or disagreeing with Shelley's view, that "Poetry subdues to union under its light yoke all irreconcilable things." [ENRIGHT, 1962, p. 252]. After discussing Eliot's relationship to Shelley [ELIOT, 1933, p. 33, 89-100, 113], it might be useful to distinguish between 1) paradox, which is content to keep two elements in permanent play and 2) contradiction, which is dialectical and seeks to reconcile things through a new perspective. 3) Which of the two do you feel to be most present in Eliot's poems? Is the poem/the work successful or unsuccessful because the 'yoking' (being made to work together) of these otherwise "irreconcilable things" is, or is not, kept 'light'? In conclusion: what aspects of Eliot's poetry does Shelley's view leave out?

As we have been dealing here with the 'serious' side of 'serious play', it is important at this critical juncture not to lose sight of the *pleasure* of reading, upon which the 'common reader' and the keeping of poetry in the common domain, depend. As an antidote to that last performative sentence, and as proof that "brevity is the soul of wit" (*Hamlet*, II, 2), we might end with Robert Frost's definition of poetry: "The figure a poem makes. It begins in delight and ends in wisdom." [HERBERT, 2000, p. 46]. The wisdom does not replace the delight; it displaces it, so that the two become intertwined, or 'interwoven', as Eliot might put it (26). Let us keep in view the essentially 'light yoke' of poetry, and not weigh it down with analysis that is too ponderous or too technical. "The worst fault that poetry can commit is to be dull" said Eliot [ELIOT, 1933, p. 52], and the same is surely true of literary criticism.

ANALYSIS

CLOSE READING OF "THE 'BOSTON EVENING TRANSCRIPT'"

The 'Boston Evening Transcript'

The readers of the *Boston Evening Transcript*
Sway in the wind like a field of ripe corn.

When evening quickens faintly in the street,
Wakening the appetites of life in some
And to others bringing the *Boston Evening Transcript*,
I mount the steps and ring the bell, turning
Wearily, as one would turn to nod good-bye to La Rochefoucauld,
If the street were time and he at the end of the street,
And I say, "Cousin Harriet, here is the *Boston Evening Transcript*."

INTRODUCTION

"The 'Boston Evening Transcript'" was written sometime before the end of May 1915, when Eliot was studying philosophy and writing his PhD on F.H. Bradley's *Appearance and Reality* at Merton College, Oxford. It was published in the same year, in the October issue of Harriet Monroe's *Poetry* magazine, and also in Ezra Pound's *Catholic Anthology*. Selected for T.S. Eliot's first published work, *Prufrock and Other Observations* (1917), it later became the sixth poem in the *Collected*

Poems. The newspaper title tells us that the poem has to do with Boston, where Eliot had lived during the years which he spent at Harvard as an undergraduate (1906-1909) and postgraduate (1910, 1912-14). With the mention of "Cousin Harriet", we are tempted to read this poem in the context of the other poems which concern Eliot's fictional Bostonian family, such as "Aunt Helen" and "Cousin Nancy", although the lateness of her appearance in the poem (in the last line) and the difference in the proper nouns of the titles (a newspaper here, rather than a person) would suggest that we might find in this poem something more than a gentle satire* of the worldview* of the Bostonian upper middle class that Eliot frequented in those years.

"The 'Boston Evening Transcript'" is the shortest poem in our selection. It is visually divided into an opening couplet, a line-space and then seven unequal lines. It will be our task to find out whether these nine lines are merely what Hamlet wearily called "Words, words, words" (*Hamlet* II, 2) or whether, arranged together, they *form* a meaning. How, for example, are the first two lines related, if at all, to the other seven? In two grammatical sentences, the "I" speaker of the poem mounts some steps and "wearily" delivers a Boston newspaper to a "Cousin Harriet". This otherwise banal event is disturbed by two thoughts in the form of images in his mind's eye: an early one of the readers of this type of newspaper, and a later one of the seventeenth-century writer La Rochefoucauld.

A poem should not mean / But be... If we are to believe the concluding words of Archibald MacLeish's "Ars poetica", commonly taken to be a manifesto of Modernist poetry, then perhaps the question we should ask ourselves is, "What *is* this poem?". In this *explication*, I will propose three inter-related answers:

– It is the dramatization of a moment.

– It is a satire on a certain type of reader.

– It is a demonstration of what poetry can do better than prose.

THE DRAMATIZATION OF A MOMENT

What makes the poem instantly recognizable as an early poem by Eliot is that it dramatizes a simple event, that of delivering a newspaper to a cousin. As befits drama, the action (the delivery of the newspaper) is set within a certain time and place, there are some *dramatis personae*, and at the end we even have the opening line of a dialogue ("Cousin Harriet, here is the *Boston Evening Transcript*.") Let us take a closer look at each of these elements in turn.

The time of the action is a recurrent one in Eliot's poems: evening, the deepening dusk, the 'violet hour' (61). It is found, though perhaps scarcely noticed, despite occurring thrice, in the title of the newspaper itself, but the word comes to life in the surprising collocation, if not actual oxymoron*, of "the evening quickens". The evening twilight, Eliot suggests here, is a dividing moment, when some set out to satisfy the "appetites of life" and others settle down to read the evening paper. At dusk, some become active ("wakening"), others passive ("bringing"). Is the division organized along gender lines? The poet does not say so, but men are (or were) commonly believed to be more driven by "the appetites of life" than women and "Cousin Harriet" is clearly female. The point is less important than the fact that the 'quickening' of evening is propitious to the writing of poetry, and congenial to the poet-persona, whose negative capability* makes it possible for him to seize the shadowy, in-between, borderline moment.

From the title of the newspaper, and our knowledge of the biographical background, we assume that the action takes place in Boston, a city which Eliot and others saw as the home of the well-bred, the easily shocked and the unexciting. Perhaps the scene is set on one of the elevated stairway entrances to the houses on Beacon Hill, the *locus* of Henry James' 'loitering occasions, wondering and invoking pauses' [JAMES, 1907, p. 230]. For it is in fact not so much the reputation of the city as the symbolic value of the staircase which Eliot wishes to evoke here.

The 'stairway moment' is a recurrent one for Eliot, as it was for Rousseau's somewhat similar *esprit d'escalier*. It is a moment of hesitation, of indecision, or regretful decision. We find it, for example, in "Time to turn back and descend the stair" in "Prufrock" (4), or in these lines from "Portrait of a Lady":

The October night comes down; returning as before
Except for a slight sensation of being ill at ease
I mount the stairs and turn the handle of the door
And feel as if I had mounted on my hands and knees. (11)

Thus, we have in "The 'Boston Evening Transcript'", in a manner typical of Eliot, a recomposing of an image from a former poem. The moment is not simply described (*I paused as I mounted the steps*) but actually performed by the unusual grammar of the poem: the freeze-frame use of present participles (*wakening, turning, bringing*) and the anachronistic, outside-time use of the present simple tense (*sway, quickens, mount, ring, say)*. The poet-persona is suspended in time (evening) and place (on the stairway), in a state of what poet Alice Oswald has called the 'arrested wakefulness' propitious to the seeing of visions and the writing of poetry.

As for the *dramatis personae*, the drama is played out among four protagonists, of whom two are, as it were, off-stage. The readers of the *Boston Evening Transcript* are apparently to be seen and not heard, though possibly they rustle in the wind that shakes the barley or, in this case, corn. In a later poem, the poet-persona joins their swaying ranks —briefly "Behaving as the wind behaves" (80)— in an attempt to escape the horror of history, but here he clearly distances himself from this anonymous mass of readers. They act as a kind of silent chorus, opening a dramatic poem which is then closed by the equally silent recipient of the newspaper, "Cousin Harriet".

Ah, Harriet. Transposing Shakespeare's question in *The Two Gentlemen of Verona* (IV, 2), we might well ask *Who is Harriet? what is she?* Is it merely a name to recall "the ariettes / Of cracked cornets" (9)? We know that she was not a real-life cousin of Eliot's, but the name 'Harriet' did have autobiographical associations. One of the amateur theatricals organized in Boston by Emily Hale and Eliot's cousin Elinor Hinkley was a dramatized version of Jane Austen's *Emma*, in which the fate of the simple and trusting Harriet Smith is tragicomically mismanaged by the blindly over-imaginative Emma (Eliot was apparently very successful in playing the role of Emma's valetudinarian father). But the name 'Harriet' might also be a, conscious or unconscious, reference to the women on whom Eliot depended for his living: Harriet Monroe and Harriet Weaver Shaw, owner-editors of *Poetry* and

The Egoist respectively. That possibility certainly fits in well with the theme we would like to develop in our second part.

And La Rochefoucauld? Of what is he the name? We know that the ever-erudite Eliot had read the *Maximes* at least, and perhaps the *Mémoires*, and in *The Sacred Wood* La Rochefoucauld is preferred to Dryden because he has a freer, more disinterested mind. But, unlike, say, the poet-rake Rochester, La Rochefoucauld is not a household name for any particular quality. So, unless Eliot is merely being pretentious —like the Lady he mocks when she says, "Without these friendships—life, what *cauchemar*!" (9)— then I do not think that his name has a metonymical function. Rather, it serves a dramatic one: he stands for any dead or receding intellectual figure to whom one says, "Hail and farewell!". In a suitably muted allusion to Swinburne's elegy to Baudelaire, the imaginary meeting between the speaker and La Rochefoucauld is to be read within the *ave atque vale* tradition.

And the speaker, the twice-mentioned 'I' of the poem? He is by no means what E.M. Forster called a 'rounded character', but rather the impersonal 'type' behind whom Eliot was fond of hiding, the ironic figure of Greek drama. This poet-persona is a variation of the Prufrock who, tongue-in-cheek, declared, "I am no prophet and here is no great matter." (6). In this poem his role is an inglorious one, that of mere delivery-boy, a parody of the Herald, or Mercury, the bringers of news, who so often appear in newspaper titles. Indeed, since in 1915 Eliot was still a free-thinker, we might see in this poem a parody of the Annunciation scene, with the poet-persona playing the role of the Angel Gabriel.

The 'action' is the delivery which does in fact happen in the poem, in the deictic 'here' of "Cousin Harriet, **here** is the *Boston Evening Transcript*." The 'prop' of that action is the newspaper itself, and it is this fact that leads us to look now at the *raison d'être* of the poem: the offering of a gentle satire on the type of reader who reads only newspapers.

A SATIRE ON A CERTAIN TYPE OF READER

Eliot's purpose in dramatizing so minor a daily event as the delivery of a newspaper is not, as might at first appear, simply to create a comic scene, a sort of prelude to a comedy of manners. It is true that the scene *is* somewhat comic, in its contrast between the philosophical and erudite poet-persona and the passive and silent (or silenced) 'Cousin Harriet' and in the bathos of the last line, "Cousin Harriet, here is the *Boston Evening Transcript*." Yet Eliot begins, we remember, not with the particular reader that is "Cousin Harriet" but with the more general "The readers". Neither reader or readers are intended as believable characters in a drama but, rather, they are *types*. Indeed, it might have been more appropriate for the poet-persona to have imagined La Bruyère at the end of the street, instead of La Rochefoucauld, but that might have been too heavy-handed an allusion, and sadly unpoetic. Similarly, it is not the eponymous *Boston Evening Transcript* that is the target of attack but a *type* of popular newspaper. For the readers, the Cousin Harriets, that Eliot has in his sights are the readers who read only newspapers.

These readers, as the quasi-epigraph of the first two lines implies, are to be seen, as Eliot and the Modernists saw them, in the mass, and possibly elderly: ripe corn. They are not reprehensible in themselves (after all, the simile is rather beautiful) but in their passive attitude to what they read: the fact that they can only "sway in the breeze", having no opinions or convictions of their own. Such readers were the antithesis of the kind of readership which the Modernist poet wished for as an audience. Being passive rather than active, they would not understand modern poetry. And, in the era of the press barons, that was indeed the case. Nor was it only a question of style only, but content too. Robert Graves went so far as to say that the only reason that the soldier-poets of World War I wrote what we now know as 'war poetry' was because they could not trust what the newspapers were reporting.

If modern poetry is seen, as it so often was, as 'too difficult' then it will not sell. The Modernist writers could not help but observe the quantitative difference between the sales of newspapers and the sales of poetry books, but the problem went beyond the commercial aspect. Critic Louise Rosenblatt, when she pointed out that newspaper-reading and poetry-reading are different experiences, was also implying that they are also different types of reading.

> Someone else can read the newspaper or a scientific work for us and summarize it acceptably. But no-one can read a poem for us. The reader of the poem must have the experience himself. [ROSENBLATT, 1938, p. 33]

The problem, Eliot's poem suggests, is one of time. Newspapers are a time-bound media *par excellence,* and the reading of them to the exclusion of all other reading will encourage a time-bound worldview, in which nothing can be imagined outside the present moment. The readers of newspapers that are sold on the streets are ill-equipped to have a vision such as the poet-persona has: "such a vision of the street / As the street hardly understands" (14). Poems, unlike newspapers, are unbound by time and can carry us backwards or forwards into the past or the future. Here, as always with Eliot, the present contains the past.

When Jeremy Irons reads this poem, he does so, brilliantly, by bringing out the irony against the newspaper world so clearly that it verges on sarcasm. A silent reading is better able to bring out the true tonality of the poem, the gentle Horatian accents of Eliot's satirical contrast between two worlds of reading. Like Ezra Pound, Eliot saw both worlds in a philosophical light. "Poetry," insisted Ezra Pound, "is news that STAYS news." And Eliot's poem shows us *how* this can be so.

A DEMONSTRATION OF WHAT POETRY CAN DO BETTER THAN PROSE

Given that newspapers are written in prose, and poems in verse, it is tempting to say, that it is that difference that makes the one easier to read than the other. Eliot would not have agreed, for he had thought long and hard about the relationship between poetry and prose. Influenced by Baudelaire's *Petits poèmes en prose* he once wrote a prose-poem*, "Hysteria" (24). In 1917 he wrote an article for the *New Statesman* interestingly entitled "The Borderline of Prose" and in *The Use of Poetry and the Use of Criticism*, he made two observations which can be retrospectively applied to our poem. First affirming that "anything that can be said as well in prose can be said *better* in prose" [ELIOT, 1933, p. 152. My emphasis]. Eliot went on to remark:

> But poetry has as much to learn from prose as from other poetry; and I like to think that an interaction between prose and verse, like the interaction between language and language, is a condition of vitality in literature. [ELIOT, 1933, p. 152]

How do these observations apply to our poem? Let us conduct an experiment to see whether what we have in verse is not better said in prose. Is our poem actually a poem and not merely prose broken up into lines? Let us look at what, if anything, happens if we lay the lines out as prose, like this:

> The readers of the *Boston Evening Transcript* sway in the wind like a field of ripe corn. When evening quickens faintly in the street, wakening the appetites of life in some and to others bringing the *Boston Evening Transcript*, I mount the steps and ring the bell, turning wearily, as one would turn to nod good-bye to La Rochefoucauld, if the street were time and he at the end of the street, and I say, "Cousin Harriet, here is the *Boston Evening Transcript*."

Clearly, the two sentences *can* be read as prose, but we soon see —as well as hear— that, read as prose, the sense becomes if anything *more* difficult to understand. But what is gained and what is lost? Although the two sentences are perfectly correct and comprehensible, grammatically speaking, the plainness we expect from prose is disrupted by several things. First, we are brought up short by the incoherence between the two sentences, whereas in the poem the *non-sequitur* is made manifest in the missing line. Then the intricacy of the second sentence becomes an irritant in the prose version, rather like the sometimes tiresomely convoluted prose of Henry James. The convolution is less irritating when arranged into seven separate lines. And finally, the present simple tense (*sways, mount, ring, says*) used to describe events in the past, which works so well in the poem, becomes disturbing in prose, for the English language, unlike the French, is not at ease with the historic present. It is our expectations of poetry, what we demand of it, as Eliot put it, that make the difference in the reception of what Eliot is saying. As Eliot once said it would, the story of Cousin Harriet and her newspaper are the lure thrown out to lull us into a state of mind in which the real poem can go to work on us. The real poem here works on the deeper levels of feeling, those of rhythm and of rhyme:

- The feeling is concentrated on that one word 'wearily'. Its placement at the beginning of the line means that the added emphasis has been gained by the *effort* of enjambment. The dactyl of *wear i ly* (looong short short) joins with the trochees (looong short) of *Bos ton, Eve ning* and *Trans cript* in a structure of falling rhythm imitating the wearisome difficulty of communication between two cousins who are worlds apart in terms of what and why they like to read.
- The internal and initial rhyme of 'sway' and 'say' is precisely that 'faint breeze of truth' which poetry brings so lightly into our lives. What do these like sounds suggest? That journalists sway, where poets say.

In conclusion, let us, intertextually, add to 'sway' and 'say' the ghost-rhyme 'stay' of Pound's "news that STAYS news". Here we have the difference between what a poet as against a reporter can make of the same banal event. It has to do with the transmission of emotion. As John Dewey put it:

> In a direct outburst an objective situation is the stimulus, the cause, of the emotion. In the poem, objective material becomes the *content and matter* of the emotion, not just its evocative occasion. [DEWEY, 1934, p. 67. My emphasis]

Here the poet-persona does not just describe the complex of emotions —weariness, discouragement, alienation— which accompany the action of delivering the newspaper: he enacts them. The poem becomes performative, on two levels. To Cousin Harriet the poet-persona wearily brings the *Boston Evening Telegraph*, the stimulus, no doubt, to yet another weary evening, and a material object to be momentarily consumed and discarded. To us, however, the poet offers a poem. What we do with it and how we read it, whether as newspaper-readers or poetry-readers, is our choice, and that is the beauty of it.

SYNTHESES AND PERSPECTIVES

ALLUSION

> In advancing the claims of a predecessor (and rotating them so that they catch a new light)
> the poet is advancing his own claims, his own poetry, and even poetry.
> [RICKS, 2002, p. 32]

It could well be said, with little fear of contradiction, that the single most important source of the novelty of Eliot's poetry is his astonishingly frequent use of the literary device of allusion. Since allusion is in itself one of the most complex and ill-defined of literary devices, Eliot's insistently allusive style might also account for the reputed difficulty of his verse. In this chapter we shall explore some of the difficulties posed by allusion, in order to understand something of *how*, but chiefly *why* a particular poet, in a particular cultural context, should choose to rely so heavily on allusion as a means of revitalizing what he saw as a dying art.

Our point of departure will, naturally, be a definition: the one provided by literary critic Earl Miner, writing in the *New Princeton Encyclopedia of Poetry and Poetics* (1993),

> Allusion is a poet's deliberate incorporation of identifiable elements from other sources, preceding or contemporaneous, textual or extratextual. [PREMINGER, 1993, p. 39]

With some help from Christopher RICKS [2002] and Linda HUTCHEON [2006], and from T.S. Eliot himself, we shall proceed to unpack this dense definition in such a way that it will serve not just to clarify our ideas about allusion in general but also to structure our argument as to why, exactly, Eliot felt the need to resort to this device more than to any other. This will involve a slight disruption of the order of the terms of the definition: we shall first develop the question of the incorporation of allusions, before turning to the question of how and by whom allusions become **identifiable** and the implications of their **provenance** (whether "preceding or contemporaneous, textual or extratextual"). Only when these issues have been addressed will we turn back to 'deliberate', the key term of the definition because it raises the issue that is central to understanding allusion: the notion of **intentionality.**

INCORPORATION

Allusions are elements taken from outside a poem and *incorporated* into it. Put another way, old wine is being put into new bottles, not an action that is proverbially recommended. Where, precisely, in the body of the new poem are the old words inserted? Conventionally at the head of the poem, in the case of a dedication or an epigraph, set apart in italics, a brooding presence which, like Banquo's ghost, is the spectre at the feast. That is quite literally true of the dedication to Jean Verdenal, the young poet with whom the young Eliot shared a pension in Paris, and who was killed in the Dardanelles: a death by drowning, as Eliot imagined it, which haunts Eliot's entire first collection, and beyond.

Elsewhere, and most frequently, the allusion is in the form of a direct quotation placed unobtrusively within the verse paragraph. The original line may be given *verbatim*, as in the last stanza of "Cousin Nancy" (22):

> Upon the glazen shelves kept watch
> Matthew and Waldo, guardians of the faith,
> The army of unalterable law.

That last line 'The army of unalterable law' is also the last line of "Lucifer in Starlight", a sonnet by George Meredith:

> On a starred night Prince Lucifer uprose.
> Tired of his dark dominion swung the fiend
> Above the rolling ball in cloud part screened,
> Where sinners hugged their spectre of repose.
> Poor prey to his hot fit of pride were those.
> And now upon his western wing he leaned,
> Now his huge bulk o'er Afric's sands careened,
> Now the black planet shadowed Arctic snows.

Soaring through wider zones that pricked his scars
With memory of the old revolt from Awe,
He reached a middle height, and at the stars,
Which are the brain of heaven, he looked, and sank.
Around the ancient track marched, rank on rank,
The army of unalterable law.

Why allude so unmistakably to Meredith's poem? One reason can be given for sure. Like Coleridge, Eliot firmly believed that poetry was "the best words in the best order" and if that was the case then any alteration of the original words would be a mark of disrespect to the original poem. A line from another poet that had lodged itself in Eliot's memory was itself inalterable: "the inexplicable line with the music which can never be recaptured in other words" [ELIOT, 1965, p. 185].

Other reasons for just that allusion in just such a poem, can of course be given but, in the absence of biographical information, and in ways that will be explored later, they must remain speculation. Does the intercourse which the allusion sets up between the two poems satirically turn Matthew Arnold and Ralph Waldo Emerson into Lucifer? Or gods? What happens when their dominion descends from the stars to the mantelpiece? What kind of ironic Awe is conferred on Nancy? Does the repetition of the last line draw attention to the fact that, unlike Meredith's, Eliot's subject, in 13 lines, cannot quite rise to the height of a sonnet? And so on. We cannot be sure of the answers to these questions, but we can discuss them, and use the answers towards what we take to be the meaning of the poem.

"Cousin Nancy" was published in *Poetry* in 1915, where not all readers enjoyed the ironic dialogue its last line set up: one accused Eliot of mere plagiarism. The accusation may well have served as an early warning to him for, even as he multiplied the number of allusions in his poems, he was careful either to offer them in fragmented form or to borrow from poets long dead. Or to use forms of allusion which could not be accused of wrong doing, such as to borrow the *form* only rather than the *words* of previous poems: the quatrain poems of his second collection do not contain quotations from Théophile Gautier's *Emaux et Camées* but they imitate the form he used. "Rhapsody on a Windy Night" borrows its jagged lines and unpredictable rhymes from Jules Laforgue. We might prefer the term 'borrow' rather than 'steal' because the later poet does give something back. We return to the older poem with new ideas and so discover new things: the dialogue really does work both ways.

RECOGNITION

Unlike commonplaces and proverbs, allusions can always be traced to a single identifiable source. "Allusion," notes Christopher Ricks, "presumes a close relation between poet and audience, a social emphasis, a community of knowledge, and a prizing of tradition, even fears of the loss of valued tradition." The incorporated element will, ideally, be both familiar to readers and yet distinctive, sustainable within tightly knit reading communities with a common cultural background and language. Perhaps the original readers of "Cousin Nancy" would have instantly recognized the allusion to the Meredith sonnet, but that would scarcely be the case today. Does that then make a poet as allusive as Eliot unreadable?

Fortunately, not, for two good reasons. On the first, all three of the critics on whom this chapter has been drawing agree. As Christopher Ricks delightfully puts it, "The allusion is a bonus, not an entrance-fee." [RICKS, 2002, p. 165]. Earl Miner adds, "The test for allusion is that it is a phenomenon that some reader or readers may fail to observe." [PREMINGER, 1993, p. 39]. Nevertheless, we understand, the poem will still work, albeit on a different level or with less nuance. And Linda Hutcheon, speaking of adaptation, which is an extended form of allusion, clinches the matter: "For an adaptation to be successful in its own right, it must be so for both knowing and unknowing audiences." [HUTCHEON, 2006, p. 121].

T.S. Eliot most surely would have agreed. Indeed, the mixed audience that he had in mind for the theatre was the same as the one he never stopped working towards in his dramatized poetry. Having divided his imaginary auditors into "the simplest", "the more thoughtful", "the more literary", "the more musically sensitive" and "auditors of greater sensitivity and understanding", he went on to declare:

> And I do not believe that the classification of audience is as clear-cut as this; but rather that the sensitiveness of every auditor is acted upon by all these elements at once, though in different degrees of consciousness. At none of these levels is the auditor bothered by the presence of that which he does not understand, or by the presence of that in which he is not interested. [ELIOT, 1933, p. 153]

The second point that should reassure the 'unknowing audience' is that the inevitable gaps in our knowledge can be easily and pleasantly filled. Indeed, the need to fill them partly accounts for the development of literary criticism and the burgeoning of English Departments, a phenomenon which was already beginning to happen in Eliot's time. As has often been remarked, the Modernists constructed the audience by whom they wished to be read. T.S. Eliot opened the way, with the "Notes" that he obligingly produced to accompany *The Waste Land*, and the fact that these may be partly tongue-in-cheek should not dismay but, on the contrary, encourage us to take a light-hearted view of literary criticism. B.C. Southam soon brought out a brief but indispensable guide to all the poems as they appeared, and nearly a century later, the annotated texts in two volumes were published, with 'commentaries' giving a wealth —almost a surfeit— of information to explain each allusion. Besides which, we have two anthologies of English poetry whose contents were chosen specifically with Eliot's work in mind: John Hayward's *Penguin Book of English Verse* (1956) and Helen Gardner's *Oxford Book of English Verse* (1972). To all these we can now add the help of the Internet search engines; indeed, it almost seems as though Eliot's allusive style announced the arrival of the hyperlink. Perhaps, as Shelley declared, poets are after all the "mirrors of the gigantic shadows which futurity casts upon the present" [ENRIGHT, 1962, p. 255].

Nor should we be surprised that this should be so. Was it not Robert Frost —a modern though not particularly allusive poet— who spoke of poetry itself in terms of re-cognition:

> For me the initial delight is in the surprise of remembering something that I didn't know I knew. [HERBERT, 2000, p. 45]

The difficulty in fact comes not from having to pay attention and to supplement our knowledge, for these are part of our being in the world, but from our uncertainty as to how much we as readers we are allowed to bring into the poem from the outside. Are there any limits to the allusions that we think we recognize, but which may be personal to ourselves?

PROVENANCE

The imported elements of an allusion, Miner's definition proclaims, come from other sources, "preceding or contemporaneous", "textual or extratextual". Of the many literary predecessors who surface in Eliot's poems, the three most important are Dante, the late Elizabethan dramatists (including the late and lesser-known plays of Shakespeare), and the Metaphysical poets. Some of the minor figures may be there to show off Eliot's erudition (for allusion also serves that purpose) but the others are such towering figures that Harold Bloom's idea of "the anxiety of influence" is by no means irrelevant here, and the critic may not be wrong who pointed out that "Allusion is a way of containing one's predecessors" [Ricks, 2002, p. 32]. The dust in "I will show you fear in a handful of dust" may be the dust of libraries, and the fear that of a sense of belatedness, of arriving too late at the party.

Allusions to work that precedes the poet assume that prior achievements are sources of value. Eliot, like Coleridge before him, harked back to what he saw as an organic and integrated society. Impatient with theories of poetry, Eliot longed to refashion a new tradition out of the old:

> In an ideal state of society, one might imagine the good New growing naturally out of the good Old, without the need for polemic and theory; this would be a society with a living tradition. [Eliot, 1965, p. 184]

It has been said that Eliot's allusions are a way of contrasting the disorder of the present with the order of the past. While this is undoubtedly true of the many allusions to Dante scattered throughout the poems and the three essays in which he discusses that religious poet, we should not be so sure of its being quite so true of the late Elizabethans. The dramatists from whom he quotes, Marlowe and Webster particularly, wrote in and about a troubled period in European history, one of religious dispute and civil war, leading up to events which loomed large in Eliot's historical worldview*: the Puritan exodus and the beheading of a king.

The contemporaneous and topical references in Eliot would appear to be less frequent and less important, structurally speaking, than the historical ones; certainly, they have been less well-studied. The allusions to *Heart of Darkness*, and particularly its brooding epigraphic presence in "The Hollow Men" (77), would suggest that more work needs to be done on the presence of Joseph Conrad (1857-1924) in the hinterland of Eliot's poems. Art, music, sculpture and dance, whether classical or modern, are only lightly alluded to but an image such as "Hakagawa, bowing among the Titians" (30) is certainly striking, and merits Ricks' fine discussion of "the energies which seethe within the line" in *T.S. Eliot and Prejudice* [RICKS, 1988, p. 123–125] to which may now be added the discovery of the actual identity of 'Hakagawa' (see webliography), and the associations (as opposed to mere prejudices) which that brings in its wake.

The difficulty and the pleasure lie in the complexity of the allusion as a literary device which, being a form of metaphor, gathers in the like and the unlike. For this reason, one of the most rewarding texts to study is the opening of "A Game of Chess" (56-57) in which the seated figure is Cleopatra, Queen Elizabeth I and Vivien Haigh-Wood, all at once. For what perhaps fascinates Eliot the most is the way in which the unity of allusion can, in broad brushstrokes, bring together on the page historical and literary moments which are unimaginably distant in time. Only allusion can perform this feat of reconstructing a new tradition out of the old, *in the poem,* out of quotations from a poet's otherwise random reading:

> Surely the great poet is, among other things, one who not merely restores a tradition which has been in abeyance, but who in his poetry re-twines as many straying strands of tradition as possible. [ELIOT, 1933, p. 85]

The tradition in question is of course that of "Tradition and the Individual Talent": not a Liberal, or Whig, tradition moving in the direction of Progress, but a classical Tory tradition, unchanging except for the occasional change of light which new talents cast upon the old. With the help of allusion, Eliot not only incorporated those parts of that tradition that he personally valued, but in so doing he incorporated himself into that tradition.

INTENTIONALITY

We come now to the most original aspect of Eliot's use of allusion: intentionality. What did Eliot intend his readers to make of some of his more obscure allusions? Let us begin with an unusual example: the mysterious figure of Phlébas, le Phénicien, or Phlebas the Phoenician who appears twice in the *Collected Poems*, in "Dans le restaurant" and "Death by Water", part IV of *The Waste Land*, respectively. Here are the two passages:

> Phlébas, le Phénicien, pendant quinze jours noyé,
> Oubliait les cris des mouettes et la houle de Cornouaille,
> Et les profits et les pertes, et la cargaison d'étain :
> Un courant de sous-mer l'emporta très loin,
> Le repassant aux étapes de sa vie antérieure.
> Figurez-vous donc, c'était un sort pénible ;
> Cependant, ce fut jadis un bel homme, de haute taille. (43-44)
> *
> Phlebas the Phoenician, a fortnight dead,
> Forgot the cry of gulls, and the deep sea swell
> And the profit and loss.
> A current under sea
> Picked his bones in whispers. As he rose and fell
> He passed the stages of his age and youth
> Entering the whirlpool.
> Gentile or Jew
> O you who turn the wheel and look to windward,
> Consider Phlebas, who was once handsome and tall as you. (65)

'Phlébus', it would seem, is the subject of a strange anecdote, perhaps from a voice overheard in a restaurant. Did Eliot intend the reader to recall the first passage in French when, within the pages of the same book, he read the second? Read as a rare occurrence of self-allusion, the second passage becomes performative of something else: in changing language, the words change in sound and tone and visual arrangement. Like Phlebus, they suffer a sea-change and metamorphose into a more beautiful image, recalling —in an added allusion— Ariel's description of Ferdinand's supposedly drowned father:

> Full fathom five thy father lies;
> Of his bones are coral made;
> Those are pearls that were his eyes;
> Nothing of him that doth fade,
> But doth suffer a sea change
> Into something rich and strange. (*The Tempest,* II, 1)

There is another, and looser, way of thinking about the relationship between the two passages: in terms not of allusion, but of intertextuality*. What is the difference between the two? Allusion, unlike intertextuality, is always intentional, or 'deliberate' as our definition has it.

With allusion, the poet steers the reader towards a meaning composed of several referents; "Gaily, when invited, beating obedient / To *controlling* hands". (69. My emphasis) With intertextuality, on the other hand, the reader is free to ignore the question of intention on the author's part, to wander freely among associations of her own choosing. The distinction is a fine one because, as Miner points out, "Allusion is also a matter of interpretation, since readers may disagree as to the deliberateness or intentionality of the incorporation of elements." [Preminger, 1993, p. 39].

What is the reader to do with allusions that are clearly personal to the poet and mysterious even to him? Eliot held that poetry was at its most intense when it was saturated with "feelings too obscure for the authors even to know quite what they were" [Eliot, 1933, p. 147]. Jean-Paul Sartre was later to take this a stage further, making the associations of a word, for both poet and reader, the very essence of poetry. The example he gave was the single word 'Florence', in an explanation so beautiful that it is worth giving here in full:

> Florence est ville et fleur et femme, elle est ville-fleur et ville-femme et fille-fleur tout à la fois. Et l'étrange objet qui paraît ainsi possède la liquidité du *fleuve*, la douce ardeur fauve de l'*or*, et, pour finir, s'abandonne avec décence et prolonge indéfiniment par l'affaiblissement continu de l'*e* muet son épanouissement plein de réserves. A cela s'ajoute l'effort insidieux de la biographie. Pour moi, Florence est aussi une certaine femme,

> une actrice américaine qui jouait dans les films muets de mon enfance et dont j'ai tout oublié, sauf qu'elle était longue comme un long gant de bal et toujours un peu lasse et toujours chaste, et toujours mariée et incompromise, et que je l'aimais, et qu'elle s'appelait Florence. Car le mot, qui arrache le prosateur à lui-même et le jette au milieu du monde, renvoie au poète, comme un miroir, sa propre image. [SARTRE, 1948, p. 21]

Eliot would surely have agreed. Every line of his poetry, charged with allusions which not only sprung from the poet's private experiences, including his reading experiences, will necessarily mean something slightly different to each individual reader who encounters them. It was as though he had taken upon himself as a poet to prove to Bertrand Russell and the Logical Atomists that their approach to the nature of language was utterly wrong: words could not be pinned down to one non-associative, purely denotational meaning. The proof would be in his poems.

Writing of adaptation which is, as we said before, an extended form of allusion, Linda spoke of "the intertextual pleasure in adaptation that some call elitist and others call enriching" [HUTCHEON, 2006, p. 117]. As readers we might well feel more comfortable in the company of the genial and expansive Walt Whitman, in whose poetry allusion plays a far smaller part. But we must take our poets as we find them, and neither Whitman nor Eliot can substitute for the other, but we can have both. Eliot was no doubt elitist by temperament and in his political outlook, but in his poetry that elitism can, if we give it leave, become enriching. In both poets, it is the poem, not the poet, which contains (with difficulty) multitudes.

A REFLECTION ON RHYME

Should I, after tea and cakes and ices,
Have the strength to force the moment to its crisis?
("The Love Song of J. Alfred Prufrock", 5-6)

Absence of rhyme is often thought of as one of the defining characteristics of modern poetry. While not wholly untrue, this idea requires considerable qualification. To begin with, we need to realize that the modern poet is by no means the first to question the use of rhyme in poetry. The English language (unlike the Italian and the French) is not rich in rhyme and the Old English poets relied on alliteration* (see below) rather than rhyme to structure their poems. Rhyme did not make an appearance in English until Chaucer, who established the heroic couplet (rhymed iambic pentameter) and the Elizabethan sonneteers, who worked with intricate patterns of rhyme. Shakespeare and Milton wrote their greatest work in blank verse (unrhymed iambic pentameter), with Milton in his preface to *Paradise Lost* being particularly disdainful of "the jingling sound of like endings". But it was John Keats who was to write the exquisite sonnet that performatively reflected on both the possibilities and the limits of rhyme:

If by dull rhymes our English must be chain'd,
And, like Andromeda, the Sonnet sweet
Fetter'd, in spite of pained loveliness;
Let us find out, if we must be constrain'd,
Sandals more interwoven and complete
To fit the naked foot of poesy;
Let us inspect the lyre, and weigh the stress
Of every chord, and see what may be gain'd
By ear industrious, and attention meet:

Misers of sound and syllable, no less
Than Midas of his coinage, let us be
Jealous of dead leaves in the bay wreath crown;
So, if we may not let the Muse be free,
She will be bound with garlands of her own.

Although he never wrote a sonnet, Eliot was to take up Keats' appeal to hear rhyme within the larger sphere of the auditory imagination*, and to see rhyme as an integral part of a poem which was self-governing, in Modernist parlance or, as Keats more sweetly said: self-garlanded.

Besides, Eliot could not completely give up rhyme insofar as he was concerned to bring the diction of modern poetry closer to ordinary speech, for ordinary speech is rife with rhyme. The primary function of rhyme is mnemonic, and so language abounds with rhymed proverbs and sayings designed to lodge folk wisdom into our memories: *Might is right, Birds of a feather flock together*... The pleasure of many stock expressions, such as *big-wig* or *dilly-dally*, depends on rhyme, which continues to proliferate in popular song: in rap in our time, and in Eliot's in the songs of Gilbert and Sullivan, the music-hall, and the Broadway comedy songs of Cole Porter. *Dilly-dally* took root in a song sung by the immensely popular music-hall star Marie Lloyd. Here is the chorus of "The Cock Linnet Song" (1919):

My old man said "Foller the van,
And don't dilly dally on the way".
Off went the van wiv me 'ome packed in it,
I walked behind wiv me old cock linnet.
But I dillied and dallied, dallied and I dillied
Lost me way and don't know where to roam.
Well you can't trust a 'special' like the old time coppers,
When you can't find your way 'ome.

As we have seen, such songs are an important feature of Eliot's poems, partly because he enjoyed them for their own sake and partly because they allow him to include the voices of the working-class audience that he would have liked to court. When Marie Lloyd died in October 1922, Eliot's unexpected and moving tribute to her art included the following shrewd and wistful observation:

> The working man who went to the music hall and saw Marie Lloyd and joined in the chorus was himself performing part of the act; he was engaged in that collaboration of the audience with the artist which is necessary in all art and most obviously in dramatic art. [ELIOT, 1932, p. 406]

That "collaboration of the audience with the artist" depended largely on the audience's perception of a rhyme pattern* which it could follow. There was of course a danger to such patterns, as Alexander Pope had once wittily pointed out:

> While they ring round the same unvaried chimes,
> With sure returns of still expected rhymes.
> Where'er you find "the cooling western breeze",
> In the next line, it "whispers through the trees":
> If "crystal streams with pleasing murmurs creep",
> The reader's threaten'd (not in vain) with "sleep".
> [ENRIGHT, 1962, p. 120]

The Modernists, as Eliot ruefully recognized, in avoiding rhyme avoided the monotony that might send an audience to sleep but without rhyme they had to work very hard to attract any audience at all.

The rhymes and repetitions of nursery rhymes, nonsense verse (Eliot was fond of Edward Lear) and the refrains in fairy tales (*Fe-fi-fo-fum / I smell the blood of an Englishman*) are the first poems we encounter as children, and we never quite forget their semi-magical power. What do we find at the very crux of *The Waste Land*, but (69) a child chanting *London Bridge is falling down falling down falling down*? In "The Hollow Men" the ironic aubade* of a child's playground game ushers in the "Falls the Shadow" lines of Part V, reputedly the most quoted passage of modern poetry of the last century:

> *Here we go round the prickly pear*
> *Prickly pear prickly pear*
> *Here we go round the prickly pear*
> *At five o'clock in the morning*. (81)

The historic meaning of these jingles heard in childhood, may now be largely lost but they can be given a new meaning in a modern context: as here, where they become a counterpoint to the story of the long-ago failure of a 'Popish plot', in Eliot's eyes a tragedy that was to have consequences that reverberated into the vacuity of the political present.

Finally, the accusation that modern verse no longer rhymes depends what is meant by 'rhyme'. As a literary term, rhyme is somewhat more complex than it might at first seem. Eliot's passing definition of rhyme as "the recurrence of identical sounds" only covers the full range of the possibilities which he himself exploited if we alter 'identical' to 'like'. It is time now to take a look at some of those possibilities of the recurrence of like sounds, which, with a nod to William Empson, will be arranged into seven groups.

SEVEN TYPES OF RHYME

Alliteration

This is also known as 'head rhyme' or 'initial rhyme'. Before the widespread use of rhyme, Old English verse, in poems such as *Beowulf,* was made memorable by the repetition of consonants. In a poem admired by Eliot, Ezra Pound brilliantly adapted "The Seafarer", an Old English poem from the Exeter Book:

> May I for my own self song's truth reckon,
> Journey's jargon, how I in harsh days
> Hardship endured oft. [POUND, 1948, p. 77]

Alliteration, or the repetition of nearby speech sounds, is the warp and woof of "Gerontion" which contains no true rhymes at all. A criss-cross of plosive consonants allows us to feel *as* we speak the old man's memories of his former hard-fought battles:

> I was neither at the ho**t** **g**a**t**es
> Nor fough**t** in the warm rain
> Nor knee **d**eep in the sal**t** marsh, heaving a **c**u**t**lass,
> **B**itten by flies, fough**t**. (29)

The plosives criss-cross with the fricatives 'f' of *fought, flies, fought* and the 'h' of *hot* and *heaving*, as they do with the repetition of *fought,* and the pauses required by two commas. When such breathing efforts are brought into play within the space of four lines, no rhyme is required!

Alliteration is an umbrella term, which covers the more specific cases of assonance and consonance. Assonance is the repetition of the same vowel sound, as in *sad* and *swam* (56). Consonance is the repetition of two consonantal sounds, with a different intervening vowel, as in *live* and *love*. Examples of consonance are hard to find in Eliot, but see the paragraph on half-rhyme, below.

Repetition

As nursery rhymes and playground chants suggest, repetition can be considered as rhyme. Repetition helps to create the 'percussion and rhythm', the persistent tom-tom which set the poet apart from the other voices otherwise threatening to drown his:

> Poetry begins, I dare say, with a savage beating a drum in a jungle, and it retains that essential of percussion and rhythm. [Eliot, 1933, p. 155]

Ever since the publication in 1913 of Gertrude Stein's poem "Sacred Emily", containing the emphatic and enigmatic line "Rose is a rose is a rose is a rose", repetition has been seen as one of the hallmarks of Modernism, but Eliot's use of repetition is both sparing and subtle, and has much to do with his abundant use of allusion (see Allusion). Take, for example, the repeated line at the end of the first part of "Ash-Wednesday". Eliot takes only part of the original Roman Catholic prayer "Hail Mary", which ends *Holy Mary, Mother of God, pray for us sinners, now and at the hour of our death*.

> Pray for us sinners now and at the hour of our death
> Pray for us now and at the hour of our death.

What the double erasure, first of "Hail Mary, Mother of God" and then of 'sinners', achieves is what he is trying to do in the poem as a whole: to transform the fixed words and truly 'unalterable law' (22) of religious belief into the fluid words that make up the poetic perception of human need.

For a secular view of a shift in repetition which enacts a shift in felt perception, we should turn back to "Prufrock" and the variable use of a comma in the reported speech of "one settling a pillow by her head" (6-7). Although it is more concerned with the proposition than the poem, this excerpt from a philosophical discussion of that strikingly repetitious passage, pins down the variation rather well:

> To Eliot, the answer to the search for meaning lies not in *definition* of "externality", but in a drama of consciousness as it encounters the phenomenal world ("Let us go and make our visit"). In the poem, one encounters a conflict or interplay between meaning as something specific, determinate, and exact, and meaning as something that is subject to the fluctuations of conscious intention, struggling to articulate itself. The speaker is uneasy with definite description. Each iteration of the search for meaning contains a slight shift: "That is not what I meant at all." becomes "That is not what I meant, at all." and "That is not it, at all." becomes "That is not it at all.". Repeating the statement *verbatim*, Eliot alters punctuation which alters, subtly, the *feeling* of the meaning. "That is not it, at all" *feels* less certain than "That is not it at all.", though the words remain identical. Eliot will replicate this technique —the use of *precisely the same words* to indicate diverse feelings— in later work. In "Prufrock", as later in *Four Quartets,* the passage of time crucially alters the experience of meaning-making, "unfixing" it from its easy resting places. [PIERCE, 2015, p. 60. Author's italics]

True rhyme

This must be on a stressed syllable, as in *macaroon/afternoon* (23), but the place of the stressed syllable in the rhyme words may vary:

Masculine (or single) rhyme falls on the last syllable: as in the opening lines of "Prufrock" (3) we have the rhymes *I / sky, streets / retreats, hotels / shells*. In fact, this early poem is a magnificent display of Eliot's virtuosity in rhyming, of which it is so replete that our attention is drawn to the very few lines which are not partnered by a rhyme. In lines 3 and 10 the last words *table* and *question* are left hanging, abandoned like the sacrificial space and the unvoiced question to which the words refer.

Feminine (or **double**) **rhyme** falls on the second-to-last syllable: platter / matter, flicker / snicker (6), sputtered / muttered (16), savannas / hosannas (42). As these examples suggest, double rhyme appears somewhat forced, and so tends towards the comic, or the ironic. The *rapprochement* effected by the rhyme *Moorgate / Margate* (64) is rather heavily ironic.

The comic effect is even more present in **triple rhyme**, which falls on the third-to-last syllable. In the following lines from "Prufrock" (7), note how through the triple rhyme of *meticulous /ridiculous*. Prufrock is turned into the almost-Fool that he fears he might well be:

> Politic, cautious, and meticulous;
> Full of high sentence but a bit obtuse;
> At times, indeed, ridiculous –
> Almost, at times, the Fool.

Rhyme usually falls on the final word of a line, but Eliot occasionally uses **initial rhyme** as in "Cousin Nancy" (22) where we find lines that, in imitation of their referent, boldly combine initial rhyme with repetition, hyperbole* and imitative punctuation:

> Miss Nancy Ellicott
> Strode across the hills and broke them,
> Rode across the hills and broke them –

In another rare case of initial rhyme, in the lines which open "A Game of Chess" (56-57), the repetition of 'glowed' serves to frame a strikingly ekphrastic* passage:

> The Chair she sat in, like a burnished throne,
> Glowed on the marble, where the glass
> Held up by standards wrought with fruited vines
> [....]
> Under the firelight, under the brush, her hair
> Spread out in fiery points
> Glowed into words, then would be savagely still.

Half-rhymes

These, which are also known as pararhymes, or slant rhymes, are oddly infrequent in Eliot's work. Perhaps this is because two strong poets, Emily Dickinson (1830-1886) and Wilfred Owen (1893-1918) had already shown their mastery of the form. Half-rhyme uses either consonance (*live / love*) or assonance (*sad /swam*). The latter half-rhyme, from "In which sad light a carvèd dolphin swam" (56) might appear trivial were it not for the fact that it unobtrusively draws together the drowned Phoenician Sailor and the Death by Water themes of an earlier and a later part.

Internal rhyme

Again, Eliot makes very sparing and discreet use of internal rhyme. An example from "The Boston Evening Transcript" (20) has already been discussed. We can find another in "The Fire Sermon" (62):

> O City city, I can sometimes hear
> Beside a public bar in Lower Thames Street,
> The pleasant whining of a mandoline
> And a clatter and a chatter from within

In the second line Eliot makes a rare relapse into prose, perhaps because of his proximity to his workplace in the City, but this is redeemed by the internal rhyme of the fourth line, which has the added advantage of being a witty allusion to "Tarentella", the poem by Hilaire Belloc which begins, "Do you remember an Inn, Miranda? / Do you remember an inn? / And the tedding and the spreading of the straw for a bedding…"

Eye-rhyme

Eye-rhyme is such a specific form of half-rhyme that it deserves to be put in a category apart. In the last lines of Keats' sonnet, we can find a fine example of eye rhyme: *crown, own*. Following Keats' advice that poets should be "Misers of sound and syllable, no less / Than Midas of his coinage", Eliot is miserly with eye-rhyme. Was this because his excellent ear found eye-rhyme too painful to contemplate? This makes the exceptional uses all the more striking, as for example the eye-rhyme of good/blood (103) of "Animula". The disjunction between the moral life of the Unitarian (good) and the ritual life of the Anglo-Catholic (blood sacrifice) raises questions which are not only autobiographical but, more profoundly, theological.

Ghost rhyme

The seventh type of rhyme is somewhat of the joker in the pack. Ghost rhyme, as its name implies, is a rhyme which is never made explicit, but which lurks behind a key word in a poem. This last type of rhyme is one which is not always recognized since, being implicit, it is to some extent speculative. It is often used to avoid the censor in ribald or scurrilous poems (of which, we remember, Eliot wrote quite a few). In such poems we should be wary of the silent rhymes to, for example, 'luck' and 'hunt'. For the *Collected Poems*, it can be useful to remain aware of the possibility of ghost rhymes partly they would fit in well with the many ghosts which feature in the poems, and partly because ghost rhyme can be an ultra-discreet, perhaps even coded, form of allusion. Eliot characteristically used the image of a ghost to dismiss the idea that modern poetry did not or should not have its own metrical pattern:

> We may therefore formulate as follows: the ghost of some simple metre should lurk behind the arras in even the 'freest' verse; to advance menacingly as we doze, and withdraw as we rouse. [ELIOT, 1965, p. 187]

Transposing this idea from metre to rhyme, I sense the ghost of some simple rhyme, in for example, the passage from "Prufrock" discussed above. Do not *meticulous* and *ridiculous* form a triple-rhyme with the unmentioned *Polonius*? And is this not why we feel Polonius must be the unnamed and suitably self-effacing referent of the "attendant lord" and not, say, the more boisterous Rosencrantz or Guildenstern? If so, why cannot Eliot quite say his name?

RHYME AND REASON

Having established that rhyme of all sorts is by no means absent from Eliot's poems, we can now admit that the modern poet nevertheless uses it sparingly. In our brief descriptions of the nature of various types of rhyme, we gave some indication of the fundamental function of rhyme. In poetry, which even on the printed page retains something of its original oral nature, "The sound must seem an Echo to the sense" [POPE, 1956, p. 67]. When rhyme is used sparingly, its every occurrence must be considered in terms of how it serves to make connections between words, whether those connections be structural, rhythmic or semantic (and often all three at once).

In traditional verse, structural rhyme follows a predictable pattern which serves to move the reader along, as she anticipates the recurrent pattern. This is true of the seven quatrain poems (32, 34, 36, 41, 45, 47, 49) although their rhyme schemes are not completely regular. In modern verse generally, where no such predictions can be made, the relative lack of rhyme slows down the reader, coaxing him into a more contemplative frame of mind. Structural rhyme serves to hold the words of a verse paragraph* together by like sounds rather than (as in prose) heavy-handed or stark grammatical rhetoric. What is true of the like sounds *within* a verse paragraph is also true of the echoes *between* paragraphs, within the poem as a whole.

While the connection between rhyme and rhythm is obvious in traditional verse, in modern poetry in which there is no regular rhyme scheme, how do the unpredictable rhymes help to create rhythm? Sometimes they do so through rather insistent repetition and anaphora, as in "There will be time…" (4) but the sign of the greatness of Eliot is that the sound patterns will often be more subtle than that. The apparently natural musicality of "Prufrock", for example, owes much to its astonishing combination of true rhyme arranged into unpredictable patterns. For those who prefer the jazzier tones of *The Waste Land*, Eliot's already fine musical ear was made even finer by Ezra Pound's selection. The highly rhythmic quality of the verse was recently made manifest by Jean-Luc Macé's setting of the poem, in the form of a dramatized reading using several voices and a musical accompaniment, alongside the written text which appeared half-line by half-line on a video screen.

Rhyme makes connections between the like sounds and (possibly) like meanings of words. We must be careful to look for differences as well as similarities. Structure can be made deliberately sound or weak, or sound in parts and weak in others. Rhythm works by point and counterpoint. Semantic connections made by like sounds can contain tensions due to for example polysemy and ambiguity. When rhyme invites comparison between two words joined by a like sound, it becomes a kind of metaphor, and so follows the rule set by Wordsworth in the preface to the *Lyrical Ballads*:

> It [the pleasure we take in metaphor] is the life of our ordinary conversation; and upon the accuracy with which similitude in dissimilitude, and dissimilitude in similitude are perceived, depend our taste and our moral feelings. [Enright, 1962, p. 180]

'Accuracy' is the key word here: we are made to *feel* the rightness of the word that is in the right place at the right time. In the first part we saw the great variety there could be in the likeness of like sounds; the same is true of the 'sense', or multiple meanings to which the like sound is attached. The play of 'like but also unlike' takes us somewhat beyond the basic principle that "the sound must seem an Echo to the sense".

In the indispensable essay entitled "Reflections on Vers Libres" (1917), from which we have already quoted, Eliot made two important points about the relative absence of rhyme in modern poetry. First, he said that the removal of rhyme made the poet work harder and thus he became more aware of the hidden resources of prose;

> The rejection of rhyme is not a leap at facility; on the contrary, it imposes a much severer strain upon the language. When the comforting echo of rhyme is removed, success or failure in the choice of words, in the sentence structure, in the order, is at once more apparent. Rhyme removed, the poet is at once held up to the standards of prose. Rhyme removed, much ethereal music leaps up from the word, music which has hitherto chirped unnoticed in the expanse of prose.

To our discussion in the "After a close reading…" chapter of Eliot's sensitivity to what poetry and prose had to offer each other, we can now add the delightful sound-image of all that once "chirped unnoticed in the expense of prose".

Secondly, Eliot went on to point out that the rarity of rhyme in modern verse conferred on it new powers when it did appear, of which he highlighted three:

> And this liberation from rhyme might be as well a liberation *of* rhyme. Freed from its exacting task of supporting lame verse, it could be applied with greater effect where it is most needed. There are often passages in an unrhymed poem where rhyme is wanted for some special effect, for a sudden tightening-up, for a cumulative insistence, or for an abrupt change of mood. [ELIOT, 1965, p. 189 Author's emphasis]

A sudden tightening-up, a cumulative insistence, an abrupt change of mood… Eliot's list is by no means exhaustive as to the possible uses of rhyme in modern verse but since it is a good start and it is his, then it is certainly worth adding to our own as, *Concordance* at hand (see Webliography) we ponder the not-so-rare rhyming words, as they occur within the context of a given poem and (perhaps) within that of the *Collected Poems* as a whole.

AFTER ELIOT

All in compassion ends
So differently from what the heart arranged:
"as well as if a manor of thy friend's..."
— Derek Walcott, "Ruins of a Great House" (1953)

The 'after' in the title of this seventh and final chapter is to be understood both literally (what came after Eliot) and figuratively (imitations of Eliot); included too in 'after' is the idea of a seeking-after, a constantly renewed and never-quite-achieved quest for 'the real Eliot', the true-true meaning of the poem. Of course, the afterlife of our selection of Eliot's poetry includes all that he himself wrote after 1930: the 'minor poems', the choruses from *The Rock*, *Four Quartets*, and the five 'occasional verses', as well as the later essays and talks, and the poetic dramas. When that considerable body of work is added to the previously uncollected —deliberately excluded— work, and once all this is re-sorted into chronological order, then one has the material for a better understanding of the development of Eliot's ideas. Our selection cuts short an overall view but, according to Hugh Haughton, that does not matter, because 1932 marks a stylistic break in Eliot's work:

> Eliot's early poetry, as evinced in poems such as "The Love-Song of J. Alfred Prufrock" and *The Waste Land*, was dramatic, lyrical, ironic and brilliantly discontinuous. His later poetry is marked by a dissociation of that precariously unified sensibility: the 'metaphysical' intelligence issued in the solemn discursiveness of *Four Quartets*, while the poetic playfulness was siphoned off into the virtuoso light verse of *Old Possum's Book of Practical Cats* (1939) and the dramatic imagination into a series of experiments in verse drama. [Hamilton, 1994, p. 148]

We note with relief that we have been given the better half: 'the dramatic, lyrical, ironic and brilliantly discontinuous' poems, written by a poet with a 'precariously unified sensibility' and a 'metaphysical intelligence', deploying together 'poetic playfulness' and 'dramatic imagination'. *Tout un programme*!

Whether one is interested in the continuity or the discontinuity of the work, one thing is sure: in 1936 Eliot's status as the leading poet of his times was established by the publication of *The Faber Book of Modern Verse*. The inclusion of the whole of *The Waste Land*, the exclusion of the war poets, and Michael Roberts' long introduction in defence of the difficulty of modern poetry, established the prestige of the Modernists for generations to come. Then, Eliot's winning the Nobel Prize in 1948 was the 'crowning privilege' of his poetic career. He wrote little poetry after that, but he used his unassailable position at Faber's to promote the work of poets very different from himself: the 'Auden generation', regional poets, protégés such as Ted Hughes and Sylvia Plath... Following Eliot's own taste, the Faber poetry list tended toward the discontinuous poetic sequence, publishing, among others, David Jones' *In Parenthesis*, Ezra Pound's *Cantos,* and Basil Bunting's *Briggflatts*. This Modernist tradition-in-the-making was later taken up by Michael Schmidt at Carcanet.

Over time the name T.S. Eliot became a kind of brand name for modern poetry in general. In 1951 Eliot set up the first and only Poetry Library, at the Southbank. The annual and prestigious T.S. Eliot prize was established by Valerie Eliot in 1993, and the T.S. Eliot Summer School in 2010. His name entered the popular Hall of Fame with Andrew Lloyd-Webber's phenomenonally successful musical *Cats*, which ran from 1981 to 2002. Woody Allen's comic extravaganza, *Midnight in Paris* (2011) would playfully conjure up the kind of artistic time travel that Eliot had recommended in more solemn mode.

On the critical front, however, Eliot's influence has met with a more mixed reception. Once again, it is Hugh Haughton who sums the situation up most cogently:

> As poet first and foremost, but also as literary and cultural critic, playwright and publisher, Eliot's influence on modern literature has been profound, controversial, and irreparable. [Hamilton, 1994, p. 149]

Haughton's decidedly ominous pronouncement was made in 1994. What did it mean, and has the situation changed in the last twenty years?

The 'profound' nature of Eliot's influence on modern poetry, is not in dispute, but that does not mean that the Modernist style has gone unchallenged. Critical debates, many of which stemmed from Eliot's own dismissals of certain of his contemporaries, flared up in the anthologies. The first concerned D.H. Lawrence, and was a plea for a less monolithic view of Modernism. Critics such as F.R. Leavis and the writers who published in the little magazine *Scrutiny*, constructed a rivalry between both the poetic vocation and the writing style of T.S. Eliot and D.H. Lawrence. In 1962 A. Alvarez made a not entirely successful bid to reconcile the two. Complaining of the 'gentility' of modern verse, Alvarez contrasted the poetry of Philip Larkin somewhat unfavourably to that of Ted Hughes. He ended an incendiary introduction to *The New Poetry* by calling for a 'new depth poetry' which would effect a reconciliation between contrasting modernisms:

> In the seriousness of what I have called the new depth poetry, the openness to experience, the psychological insight, and integrity of D.H. Lawrence would, ideally, combine with the technical skill and formal intelligence of T.S. Eliot. If this were to happen we would have contemporary work which, like Coleridge's Imagination, would reconcile 'a more than usual state of emotion with a more than usual order'. [ALVAREZ, 1962, p. 32]

At the same time as a critical opposition was being constructed between Eliot and Lawrence, a different case was being made for the reinstatement of Thomas Hardy (1840-1928). As early as 1936 Ian Parsons at Chatto & Windus, a rival publishing-house to that of Faber's, brought out an anthology designed to broaden the Faber view of modern verse. Even the title *The Progress of Poetry, from Hardy to the present day* announced that it would include poets that were considered more reader-friendly than the Modernists. In the 1950s another anthology, *New Lines*, introduced the 'Movement', a new generation of poets who disliked the grandiloquence of both the Modernists and the New Romantics. The best of the poets in the Movement, a term which he disliked, was Philip Larkin. When in 1973 Larkin published *The Oxford Book of Twentieth-Century English Verse*, his choice shocked the *literati*, though not perhaps the common readers, of poetry. Eliot was among the poets chosen, but his American friends were not. In Larkin's homegrown tradition, the poet who was given pride of place was not Eliot, but Thomas Hardy. In the hands of later critics, the rivalry soon hardened into a tale of two traditions: the Modernist and the anti-Modernist.

Is the construction of such rivalries between poets either necessary or useful? It may well be necessary for the anthologist in need of a good reason for his exclusions and it can sometimes provide an entry-point for the literary critic in search of an argument, but I do not think that the common reader gains much benefit from these make-believe quarrels. Comparison, as we suggested before, does help analysis, but it does not have to promote one at the expense of the other for, as Eliot himself insisted, "Nothing in this world or the next is a substitute for anything else." [ELIOT, 1933, p. 113]. Why should we not enjoy, in different moods and for different reasons, alongside *The Waste Land*, Hardy's plangent *Poems of 1912-1913 and* "Poetry of the Present", Lawrence's magnificent introduction to *New Poems* (1920)?

In short and long time, our needs change, as Eliot once remarked:

> No generation is interested in Art in quite the same way as any other; each generation, like each individual, brings to the contemplation of art its own categories of appreciation, makes its own demands on art, and has its own uses for art. [ELIOT, 1933, p. 109]

Recent trends in literary criticism have directed attention away from literary squabbles and towards the relationship between literature and place. Place and literature feature even in the title of Robert Crawford's recent biography, *Young Eliot: From St. Louis to The Waste Land*. The trend sometimes takes a transatlantic turn, as though following the sea-voyage imagined by Bob Dylan in the very year of Eliot's death:

> Praise be to Nero's Neptune
> The Titanic sails at dawn
> And everybody's shouting
> "Which Side Are You On?"
> And Ezra Pound and T. S. Eliot
> Fighting in the captain's tower
> While calypso singers laugh at them

And fishermen hold flowers
Between the windows of the sea
Where lovely mermaids flow
And nobody has to think too much
About Desolation Row

Inspired by the multilingual allusions in Eliot's poems, critics have also been looking at the connections to be made between his poetry and the poets of the Indian Empire: Rabindranath Tagore (1861-1941) for example. They have also journeyed in search of wherever Eliot might have located what he called the 'European mind': Greece, Germany, Italy, France...

The French connection is obviously one that interests us, especially because it implies an interest in translation. Pierre Leyris' 1947 translation of Eliot's poems has very recently been joined by those, amongothers, of Michel Vinaver and Monique Lojkine-Morélec. (s. Webliography). And thinking thematically, questions abound: about Eliot's 1909 residence in France and his many visits after that, his literary friendships, his connections to the philosophy of Bergson and to the politics of Maurras...

A good place to start would be the book of essays recently edited by Jayme Stayer, not least for the preface by William Marx, in which he ponders the astonishing neglect of the clearly Francophile Eliot in France, for which he finds four reasons. He begins by ruefully admitting that "Since the time of Mallarmé, poetry has become less and less popular in France and is perceived as a plaything for connoisseurs." [Stayer, 2015, p. xi]. Adding that Eliot was unfortunate in choosing Le Seuil and not Gallimard as his publisher, he goes on to point out that the French perspective on Modernism tends to ignore the Anglo-American tradition in favour of Surrealism. His last point is surely the most interesting of all, in what it says of the French discomfort with the religious tenor of some of Eliot's work. He argues that the success of the Gallicanism in France led to an aesthetic movement in the second half of the nineteenth century in which literature and the doctrine of aestheticism became the new religion. Eliot, however much he admired the Symbolists who incarnated this worldview, remained strongly opposed to the replacement of religion by literature. The conclusion to W. Marx's argument provides much food for thought:

> For a French reader, Christian writers can only be traitors at best, if not frauds. Since their work refers to a sacredness other than its own, they cannot be taken seriously as writers. The disapproval of any Christian literature has less to do with anticlericalism than with the French overvaluation of literature in the last two centuries. [STAYER, 2015, p. XIII]

So much, then, for the profundity and extent of interest in Eliot's early work since his death in 1965. But what, in the context of a civil service exam. and in the short space available here, can be said of what Haughton calls its 'controversial' nature? Only a few brief points can be made.

There are three main areas of controversy: Eliot's homosexuality, his misogyny, and his anti-Semitism. In all three cases, it is possible to defend Eliot on historical grounds: to argue that Eliot's view was not a personal one, but part of the worldview current at the time. This is truer of Eliot than most, given his view that "Poetry is not a turning loose of emotion, but an escape from emotion; it is not an expression of personality but an escape from personality." [HERBERT, 2000, p. 38]. Presumably this also implies that such poetry will be a more than usual reflection not of the man but the *Zeitgeist*. Yes, but... The historical argument is not totally satisfactory.

The spirit of our times, Western notions of right and wrong, have changed a lot since those of Eliot. Before 1967, homosexuality was a crime in England, whereas anti-semitism was not. Now it is the other way around. So, when Eliot was accused of homosexuality in an article in the 1950s, it is not surprising that he reacted violently and did his best to suppress it. Since then, one of his biographers has argued from rather slim evidence that Eliot was a not very repressed homosexual. If that is the case, then no doubt we can expect critics cognizant in Queer Theory to read the poems in a different light.

Only the legal status of misogyny has not changed, which is interesting because it is certainly not hard to argue that Eliot feared, if he did not actually hate or despise, women, whilst at the same time enjoying their company. Lyndall Gordon's latest biography, *The Hyacinth Girl*, is not only about the long-hidden affair with Emily Hale; it is also shrewd about Eliot's other relationships with women. So, the field is open to feminist critics to use the biographical facts as a basis for new readings of the work.

For both questions, it is pertinent to ask whether it is possible to separate the man from the work. For the reason given above, the French are not unduly inclined to find fault with the work because of the sins of the man. English-speaking readers tend to be more Puritan on that count, a characteristic which has not diminished with the now widely current 'cancel-culture'. It is not always difficult to separate the two. Just as we try to judge not a person but their behaviour so we should not presume to judge the poet but we are free to judge the poem. And on the question of judgement, Christopher Ricks in *T.S. Eliot and Prejudice* wittily develops two ideas: that no-one, least of all literary critics, is free from prejudice, and that the overhasty and sometimes violent readings that prejudice provokes are rarely either elegant or helpful.

Eliot's anti-Semitism is a graver matter, with the most egregious examples being found on pages 29, 32-33, 49 of the *Collected Poems*. The issue was first raised publicly by Emanuel Litvinoff (1915-2011), a poet from the East End of London, the area of London nearest the docks and which had been most heavily bombed during the war. Serving in Africa, he had written, in vain, a number of poems during the war to draw attention to the plight of the Jews in Occupied Europe. Shocked when Eliot re-selected "Gerontion" (29), "Burbank with a Baedeker: Bleistein with a Cigar" (32-33) and "Sweeney among the Nightingales" (49) for republication in the *Selected Poems* of 1948, he wrote his own poem, "To T.S. Eliot" and read it out, with T.S. Eliot present in the audience, at the opening of the Institute of Contemporary Arts. The audience erupted, Stephen Spender protested, but Eliot himself, getting up to leave, was heard to mutter, "It's a good poem. It's a very good poem." Here it is:

To T.S. Eliot
Eminence becomes you. Now when the rock is struck
your young sardonic voice which broke on beauty
floats amid incense and speaks oracles
as though a god
utters from Russell Square and condescends,
high in the solemn cathedral of the air,
his holy octaves to a million radios.
I am not one accepted in your parish.
Bleistein is my relative and I share
the protozoic slime of Shylock, a page

in Stürmer, and, underneath the cities,
a billet somewhat lower than the rats.
Blood in the sewers. Pieces of our flesh
float with the ordure on the Vistula.
You had a sermon but it was not this.
It would seem, then, yours is a voice
remote, singing another river
and the gilded wreck of princes only
for Time's ruin. It is hard to kneel
when knees are stiff.
But London Semite Russian Pale, you will say
Heaven is not in our voices.
The accent, I confess, is merely human,
speaking of passion with a small letter
and, crying widow, mourning not the Church
but a woman staring the sexless sea
for no ship's return,
and no fruit singing in the orchards.
Yet walking with Cohen when the sun exploded
and darkness choked our nostrils,
and the smoke drifting over Treblinka
reeked of the smouldering ashes of children,
I thought what an angry poem
you would have made of it, given the pity.
But your eye is a telescope
scanning the circuit of stars
for Good-Good and Evil Absolute,
and, at luncheon, turns fastidiously from fleshy
noses to contemplation of the knife
twisting among the entrails of spaghetti.
So shall I say it is not eminence chills
but the snigger from behind the covers of history,
the sly words and the cold heart
and footprints made with blood upon a continent?
Let your words
tread lightly on this earth of Europe
lest my people's bones protest.

Part of the beauty of the story is that the repeated 'it' of Eliot's muttered comment is ambiguous: "It's a good poem. It's a very good poem." Was he twice defending his own poem, or Litvinoff's, or was he defending both, in ascending order of merit?

What to do with what we now call 'hate speech'? In the last chapter of *Religion and Science*, Russell defines ethical values as desires for whatever each person subjectively defines as 'the Good'. Such definitions, he argues, lie outside the domain of scientific knowledge: 'That is to say, when we assert that this or that has 'value' we are *giving expression to our own emotions*, not to a fact which would still be true if our personal feelings were different.' From this it follows that, 'Every attempt to persuade people that something is good (or bad) in itself, and not merely in its effects, depends upon *the art of arousing feelings*, not upon an appeal to evidence.' For Russell, there are no purely scientific arguments in favour of either democracy or fascism, nor can you change the minds of Fascists or Democrats by an appeal to scientific evidence but, he affirms, there *are* emotional ways of altering men's opinions on such subjects. [RUSSELL, 1935, p. 230, 235. My italics].

T.S. Eliot thought that literary criticism could tell us what and how much to feel about 'controversial' subjects. But, following Russell, we are entitled to ask whether, rather than counter an unethical poem by rational criticism, we let a poem drive out a poem? Or stand alongside it, in telling —situated and embodied— contrast?

If we let poems answer poems, then we come back to that central concern in Eliot's poetry, allusion. What happens when later poets, Eliot-like, allude to Eliot's work? The answer depends on the form of the later poem, and on its tone. Let us mention and look at excerpts from a few examples, all of them from poets published by Faber. The first two are in the mode of parody, which Linda Hutcheon defined as "imitation characterized by ironic inversion, not always at the expense of the parodied text". In "A Drunk Man Looks at a Thistle" (1925) Hugh MacDiarmid offered a satirical and Scottish take on Eliot's solemnity and Dantean themes. The second, because it reduces Eliot's epic to the Lilliputian proportions of a limerick, could even be called pastiche. Here is the first of Wendy Cope's five "Waste Land Limericks":

In April one seldom feels cheerful;
Dry stones, sun and dust make me fearful;
Clairvoyantes distress me,
Commuters depress me—
Met Stetson and gave him an earful.

Three further examples strike a more serious note, so clearly yet lightly allusive that, like Eliot's own, they become poems in their own right, independent of Eliot, yet each in their various ways paying homage to a great predecessor. Copyright considerations prevent me from quoting them here, but they are available on the Internet and deserve to be savoured at leisure. Stevie Smith's "Not Waving but Drowning", one of the most famous of modern poems, can be read in the reciprocal light of "Phlebus the Phoenician". In "Ruins of a Great House" the then young Derek Walcott's relationship to Eliot is like that of the young Eliot's to Henry James in "Portrait of a Lady", a meeting of masters of language. Tony Harrison's "A Cold Coming" borrows from Eliot's "Journey of the Magi" to make a brilliantly savage attack on the first Gulf War.

Finally, since it is freely available at Poetry International online, we might quote in full Seamus Heaney's tribute to Ted Hughes and his mentor T.S. Eliot. Playfully serious, it encapsulates the continuity of individual talents and a modern tradition:

Stern
'And what was it like,' I asked him,
'Meeting Eliot?'
　　　　　　'When he looked at you,'
He said, 'it was like standing on a quay
Watching the prow of the Queen Mary
Come towards you, very slowly.'

　　　　　　Now it seems
I'm standing on a pierhead watching him
All the while watching me as he rows out
And a wooden end-stopped stern
Labours and shimmers and dips,
Making no real headway.

In conclusion, what can we say in reply to Hugh Haughton's idea that Eliot's influence on the modern tradition was not only 'profound' and 'controversial' but also 'irreparable'? Once again, it might be best to let a poet answer a poet. Alice Oswald's last two lectures as Oxford Professor of Poetry were both about T.S. Eliot. In the first, having moved to Bristol from her garden in Devon in order to absorb the urban atmosphere she deemed indispensable for a rereading-rewriting of The Waste Land, she takes "A distracted walkabout with T.S. Eliot and others". In the second, she draws mock-serious inspiration from *Blast* and other Modernist manifestos and calls for a return of the rhapsode.

> Manifesto for stitchwork written
> in retrospect for the rhapsodes.
> Rhapsody is a similest movement that
> is dedicated to studying, repairing,
> speaking, patching up, unlearning and
> mending. Our Manifesto is for the small
> words of the great poems by means of which
> multiple minds may be stitched together.

This small excerpt will serve to show that, for this pre-eminent contemporary poet, Eliot and his like have done no damage so great that it cannot be mended. The rhapsodes are ready: it is their task to stitch together the "small / words" of "the great poems" into what might become an epic *Collective Poems* of the future.

WEBLIOGRAPHY

Obviously, given the restraints of print publication, these pages cannot connect via hyperlinks to the online resources described. These merely descriptive Internet notes are offered in the spirit of a checklist, with a view to saving precious time for students. The words used for each resource, if typed into Google, will take them very quickly to the referenced page.

GENERAL RESOURCES

Internet Archive: all the books mentioned in the Bibliography can be borrowed from here.

Poetry Foundation: the home of Harriet Monroe's *Poetry* magazine, with all the issues, going back to 1912. + a wealth of other resources.

Representative Poetry Online: another searchable and rich resource.

Poets.org: a rich resource from the Academy of American Poets.

Modernist Journals Project: a free and searchable archive of digital scans of 'little magazines'.

Discovering Literature: these British Library webpages offer resources for reading key works in context.

The T.S. Eliot Estate at Faber and Faber: probably all you will need to know about Eliot and his world, including the Emily Hale letters, essays, lectures and many other resources.

The PennSound webpage: for vintage recordings of Eliot reading his own poetry.

INTERNET NOTES

Acknowledgements

Several of Christopher Ricks' lectures on T.S. Eliot are available on YouTube.

Foreword

Older printings of the *Collected Poems* can be downloaded from Internet Archive. This can be a useful for searching for the source of a line, or checking out further occurrences of a word. A *Concordance to the Complete Poems and Plays* is available at Internet Archive.

Introduction: The Art of Reading

I recommend Marcel Proust's "Sur la lecture" (1905), which is free to access on the Internet.

A Portrait of a Poet

Paul Gauguin's *Le Christ Jaune* (1889) has a 'twin' painting: *Autoportrait au Christ jaune* (1891).

There is a rather good description of Mannerism at The Art Story: "Artists in 16th-century Florence and Rome started to veer from classical influences and move toward a more intellectual and expressive approach. This ushered in a veer from authentic portrayals of figures and subjects, a rejection of harmony, and the development of a dramatic new style unconfined by the pictorial plane, reality, or literal correctness. Radical asymmetry, artifice, and the decorative also informed this movement. New discoveries in science had led society away from Humanist ideals and paintings no longer posited man as the center of the universe, but rather as isolated, peripheral participants in the great mysteries of life."

The Church of St. Magnus Martyr, near London Bridge, has a webpage which offers a virtual tour, in which one can see the white and gold splendour of its Wren interior.

A Sketch of an Age

Marcel Duchamp's second painting (1912) of a *Nude Descending a Staircase* can be viewed at the Philadelphia Museum of Art.

There are several good documentaries on John Singer Sergeant (1856-1925) and Walter Sickert (1860-1942) on YouTube.

Wyndham Lewis's 1938 portrait of Eliot, refused by Royal Academy was sold to Durban Art Gallery. Eliot commented, "It seems to me a very good portrait, and one by which I am quite willing that posterity should know me, if it takes any interest in me at all and I certainly have no desire, now, that my portrait should be painted by any painter whose portrait of me would be accepted by the Royal Academy. (Letter to Wyndham Lewis, April 21, 1938)

The Wiki page on Post-Impressionism is very lively and quite complete.

Paul Nash's *The Menin Road* (1919) can be seen in the Imperial War Museum's collection.

Short documentaries and the music of William Walton's *Façade* (1922), Erik Satie's *Parade* (1917), Igor Stravinsky's Rite of Spring (1913, 1920), and Ralph Vaughan Williams' *Fantasia on a Theme by Thomas Tallis* (1910), *The Lark Ascending* (1914), and *Pastoral Symphony* (1922) are available on YouTube.

Towards a Theory of the Art of Poetry

Shelley's "A Defence of Poetry" is available from Wikisource.

A close reading of "The Boston Evening Transcript" (1915)

The *Boston Evening Transcript* was a daily afternoon newspaper in Boston, Massachusetts, published 1830-1941, appearing daily except Sunday. It ran feature articles, published poems, and was particularly appreciated for its obituaries, a detail which provides another link to Joyce's short story "The Dead" in *Dubliners*.

Allusion

Jeffrey Meyers has written a recent essay on "The Shock of Recognition: Conrad's Influence on Eliot" but it is currently behind a paywall.

For more on 'Hakagawa' see Frances Dickey's page "On Pictures" at the T.S. Eliot Society.

Rhyme

Wikisource provides Edmund Gosse's article on "Rhyme", from the 1911 Encyclopedia Britannica, reputedly the finest edition of that work, and one Eliot might have known.

After Eliot

Wendy Cope wrote five limericks in all, one to summarize each part of *The Waste Land*. They are hilarious.

Stevie Smith's "Not waving but drowning" can be found at the Poetry Foundation.

Podcasts, videos and transcripts of Alice Oswald's lectures as Oxford Professor of Poetry are available from Oxford university and YouTube. "The Life and Death of Poetry: A distracted walkabout with T.S. Eliotand Others" and "Counterblast! (a manifesto for poetry)" are particularly relevant.

BIBLIOGRAPHICAL REFERENCES

An official bibliography is available from the T.S. Eliot website, and from this a select bibliography has been designed especially for the *agrégation*. The primary function of what follows here is to provide the references for quotations and works alluded to in the main part of the text. In addition, the references to works contemporary with the period 1910-1936, viewed collectively, gain a secondary function, which is to offer a 'rickety and ramshackle' guide to Eliot's worldview.

ABERCROMBIE, L. *Principles of Literary Criticism*. London, Victor Gollancz, 1932.

ACKROYD, P. *T.S. Eliot*. London. Sphere Books, 1988.

ADAMS, H. *The Education of Henry Adams: An Autobiography*. Boston, Houghton Mifflin Company, 1918.

ALVAREZ, A. *The New Poetry*. Harmondsworth, Penguin Books, 1962.

ARNOLD, M. *Culture and Anarchy: An Essay in Political and Social Criticism*. [1869] Cambridge, Cambridge University Press, 1932.

ARNOLD, M. *Essays in Criticism: Second Series*. [1888] London, The Macmillan Company, 1913.

AUDEN, W.H. *The Dyer's Hand*. London, Faber and Faber, 1963.

AUSTIN, J.L. *How to Do Things with Words*. Cambridge, Harvard University Press, 1962.

BACHELARD, G. *L'Eau et les rêves : Essai sur l'imagination de la matière*. Paris, Éd. Corti, 1942.

BALDICK, C. *The Oxford Dictionary of Literary Terms*. Oxford, Oxford University Press, 2015.

BAUDELAIRE, C. *Œuvres complètes*, Paris, Éditions Gallimard, 2001.

BELL, C. *Art*. New York, Frederick A. Stokes Company, 1913.

BODKIN, M. *Archetypal Patterns in Poetry: Psychological Studies of the Imagination*. Oxford, Oxford University Press, 1934.

BRADLEY, A.C. *Oxford Lectures on Poetry*. London, Macmillan & Company, 1909.

BRADLEY, F.H. *Appearance and Reality: A Metaphysical Essay*. London, George Allen and Unwin, 1893.

BUTLER, C. *Modernism: A Very Short Introduction*. Oxford: Oxford University Press, 2010.

CHILDS, P. *Modernism*. London, Routledge, 2000.

CHURCHILL, W. *The World Crisis*. 6 vols. London, Thornton Butterworth, 1923-1931.

CRAWFORD, R. *Young Eliot: From St. Louis to The Waste Land*. New York, Macmillan, 2015.

DEWEY, J. *Art as Experience*. New York, Minton, Balch & Company, 1934.

EMERSON, R.W. "Poetry and Imagination", *The Complete Works of Ralph Waldo Emerson*. Vol. 8. Boston, Houghton Mifflin Company, 1917.

ELIOT, T.S. *The Sacred Wood: Essays on Poetry and Criticism*. London, Methuen and Company, 1920.

ELIOT, T.S. *Selected Essays, 1917-1932*, London, Faber and Faber, 1932.

ELIOT, T.S. *The Use of Poetry and the Use of Criticism*. London, Faber and Faber, 1933.

ELIOT, T.S. *Collected Poems 1909-1962*. London, Faber and Faber, 1963.

ELIOT, T.S. *To Criticize the Critic and Other Writings*. London, Faber and Faber, 1965.

ELIOT, V. ed. *The Letters of T.S. Eliot Vol 1, 1898-1922*. New York, Harcourt Brace Jovanovich, 1988.

EMPSON, W. *Seven Types of Ambiguity*, London, Chatto and Windus, 1930, 1947.

ENRIGHT, D.J. and E. De Chickera, *English Critical Texts*. Oxford, Clarendon Press, 1962.

FENTON, J. *An Introduction to English Poetry*. London, Penguin Books, 2003.

FORSTER, E.M. *Howard's End*. London, Edward Arnold, 1910.

GARDNER, H. *In Defence of the Imagination*. Cambridge, Mass., Harvard University Press. 1982.

GIFFORD, H. *Poetry in a Divided World: The Clark Lectures 1985*. Cambridge, Cambridge University Press, 1985.

GISSING, G. *New Grub Street*. [1891] London, Penguin Books, 1968.

GRAVES, R. *On English Poetry*. New York, Alfred A. Knopf, 1922.

GROSS, J. *The Rise and Fall of the Man of Letters: Aspects of English Literary Life since 1800*. London, Penguin Books, 1973.

HAMILTON, I. ed. *The Oxford Companion to Twentieth-Century Poetry in English*. Oxford, Oxford University Press, 1994.

HARDY, T. *Collected Poems*. London, Macmillan and Company, 1923.

HARGROVE, N.D. *T.S. Eliot's Parisian Year*. Gainsville, University Press of Florida, 2009.

HAYWARD, J. *The Penguin Book of English Verse*. London, Penguin Books, 1956.

HERBERT, W.N. & M. Hollis, ed. *Strong Words: Modern Poets on Modern Poetry*. Newcastle, Bloodaxe Books, 2000.

HERCEND, O. and K. K. Toda ed. *T. S. Eliot. Collected Poems 1909-1962*, *Agrégation anglais 2024*, Paris, Ellipses, 2023.

HUTCHEON, L. *A Theory of Parody: The Teachings of Twentieth-Century Art Forms*. Champaign, University of Illinois Press, 2000.

HUTCHEON, L. *A Theory of Adaptation*. London, Routledge, 2006.

HULME, T.E. *Speculations: Essays on Humanism and the Philosophy of Art*. ed. Herbert Read, London, Kegan Paul, Trench, Trubner and Co., 1924.

HYNES, S. *The Auden Generation: Literature and Politics in England in the 1930s*. London, Faber and Faber, 1976.

JAMES, H. *Portrait of a Lady*. New York, Macmillan and Company, 1881.

JAMES, H. The Bostonians. New York, Macmillan and Company, 1887

JAMES, H. *The Real Thing and Other Stories*. New York, Macmillan and Company, 1893.

JAMES, H. *The American Scene*. London, Chapman and Hall, 1907.

JOYCE, J. *Dubliners*. London, Grant Richards Ltd., 1914.

LARKIN, P. *Collected Poems*. London, Faber and Faber, 1988.

LAWRENCE, D.H. *New Poems*. London, W. Huebsch, 1920.

PARSONS, I.M. *The Progress of Poetry: An Anthology of Verse from Hardy to the Present Day*, London, Chatto & Windus, 1936.

PHILIPPE, C-L. *Bubu de Montparnasse*. Trans. L. Vail, with a preface by T.S. Eliot. Paris, Crosby Continental Editions, 1932.

PIERCE, A.E. *Of Poems and Propositions: T.S. Eliot and the Linguistic Turn*, D. Hil, Oxford, 2015.

POPE, A. *Collected Poems*. London, Everyman's Library, 1956.

POUND, E. *Selected Poems*. ed. T.S. Eliot. London, Faber and Faber, 1928, 1948.

POUND, E. *Literary Essays of Ezra Pound*. ed. T.S. Eliot. New York, New Directions, 1936.

PRATT, M-L. *Towards a Speech Act Theory of Literary Discourse*. Bloomington, Indiana University Press, 1977.

PREMINGER, A. and BOGAN T.V.F., *The New Princeton Encyclopedia of Poetry and Poetics*. Princeton, Princeton University Press, 1993.

RICKS, C. *T.S. Eliot and Prejudice*. Berkeley, University of California Press, 1988.

RICKS, C. *Allusion to the Poets*. Oxford, Oxford University Press, 2002.

RICKS, C. and MCCUE J., ed. *The Poems of T. S. Eliot: The Annotated Text*. London, Faber and Faber, 2015.

RIDING, L. and R. Graves. *A Survey of Modernist Poetry*. New York, Doubleday, Doran and Company, 1928.

ROBERTS. M. *The Faber Book of Modern Verse*. London, Faber and Faber, 1936.

ROBINS, A.G. *Modern Art in Britain, 1910-1914*. London, Barbican Art Gallery, 1997.

ROSENBLATT, L.M. *Literature as Exploration*. New York, Appleton-Century Company, 1938.

RUSSELL, B. *Mysticism and Logic and Other Essays*. London, George Allen and Unwin, 1917.

RUSSELL, B. *Religion and Science*. London: Thornton Butterworth Ltd., 1935.

RUSSELL, B. *Why I am not a Christian and Other Essays on Religion and Related Subjects*. New York, Simon and Schuster, 1957.

SARTRE, J-P. *Qu'est-ce que la littérature ?* Paris, Gallimard, 1948.

SCHMIDT, M. *Lives of the Poets*. London, Orion Books, 1998.

SOUTHAM, B.C. *A Student's Guide to the Selected Poems of T.S. Eliot*. London, Faber and Faber,1968.

STAYER, J. *T.S. Eliot, France and the Mind of Europe*, Newcastle, Cambridge Scholars Publishing, 2015.

STEIN, G. *Geography and Plays*. Boston, The Four Seas Company, 1922.

STEPHENSON, B. *Ritual: A Very Short Introduction*, Oxford, Oxford University Press, 2015.

SYMONS, A. *The Symbolist Movement in Literature*. London, E.P. Dutton and Company, 1899, 1919.

TAGORE, R. *Œuvres*. Éd. F. Chartier. Paris, Gallimard, 2020.

TILLYARD, E.M.W. *The Elizabethan World Picture*. London, Chatto and Windus, 1943.

VALÉRY, P. *La Crise de l'esprit, suivi de Note (ou L'Européen)*. Paris, Éd. Manucius, 2016.

WAUGH, E. *Brideshead Revisited: The Sacred and Profane Memories of Captain Charles Ryder*. London, Chapman and Hall, 1945.

WHEELWRIGHT, P. *The Burning Fountain: A Study in the Language of Symbolism*. Bloomington, University of Indiana, 1968.

WHITMAN, W. *Leaves of Grass*. New York, Norton and Company, 1973.

WILSON, E. *The Shores of Light: A Literary Chronicle of the Twenties and Thirties,* New York, Farrar, Strauss and Giroux, 1952.

WOOLF, V. *Monday or Tuesday*. New York, Harcourt, Brace & Co, 1921.

WOOLF, V. *The Common Reader*. New York, Harcourt, Brace & Co, 1925.

YEATS, W.B. *Essays and Introductions*. London, Macmillan and Company, 1961.

GLOSSARY

The following glossary of literary terms has been compiled with a view to its usefulness for the study of T.S. Eliot's poems up to 1932. The definitions have been adapted from various dictionaries of literary terms, including those of M.H. Abrahms, and Chris Baldick, as well as the unsigned one available online at the Poetry Foundation. To the succinct definitions have been added a few examples from the *Collected Poems*, but the idea is for students to seek out their own.

addressee: the person to whom a poem is implicitly or explicitly addressed. Ex: Part II of Ash-Wednesday (87-88) begins, "Lady,". Who is this 'lady'? Emily Hale? The Lady of 'Portrait of a Lady'? The Virgin Mary? Beatrice? The Muse? La Belle Dame sans merci? A personification of some human quality? All, some or none of these? What effect is lost or gained if this single word is omitted? The answers to these questions will affect the overall **tone** and therefore the interpretation of this part of the poem.

allegory: a story in which everything (especially plot and character) corresponds on two levels, the literal and the figurative. Allegory can be historical, political, religious or philosophical. Literary critic Hugh Haughton considers "Gerontion" to be a "cunningly contrived historical allegory" [HAMILTON, 1994, p. 147].

alliteration: repetition of initial sounds. See the "Rhyme" chapter.

allusion: a reference, explicit or implicit, to a person, place, event, or another literary work. See the "Allusion" chapter.

ambiguity: an openness to multiple interpretations, a deliberate imprecision. See **negative capability**. cf. William Empson, in *Seven Types of Ambiguity* (1930).

anaphora: ("carrying back") the same word or groups of words repeated at the beginning of successive lines.

anxiety of influence: for a poet, a literary, as opposed to an historical, source of anxiety. Harold Bloom, in *The Anxiety of Influence* (1973) declared that "the covert subject of most poetry for the last three centuries has been the anxiety of influence, each poet's fear that no proper work remains for him to perform." In such a view, Eliot's work can be read as a reaction to (say) the democratic views of Walt Whitman and, more precisely, to the various views of those whom he might have admitted to be his contemporary equals: Thomas Hardy, Ezra Pound, Robert Frost, W.B. Yeats...

archetype: J.G. Frazer's *The Golden Bough* (1890-1915) found elemental patterns in the myths and rituals of societies widely dispersed in time and space. TSE acknowledged his debt to Frazer in the notes to *The Waste Land* (70), as well as to Jessie Weston's *From Ritual to Romance* (1920). The latter emphasized the persistence of versions of legends of the Holy Grail in and beyond the Arthurian legends, and the Celtic myth that linked a barren land with a curse that must be lifted by a hero. Her work was developed by anthropologists such as Lucien Lévy-Bruhl and psychiatrists such as Carl Jung. Maud Bodkin applied some of these ideas in *Archetypal Patterns in Poetry* (1934).

ars poetica: an explanation by a poet, often in verse, of that poet's theory of poetry. The best-known twentieth-century *ars poetica* is that of Archibald MacLeish, which ends "A poem should not mean / But be."

assertorial weight: a not very elegant, but useful, term coined by Philip Wheelwright to describe the necessary *lightness* of poetry. Where prose asserts, poetry suggests. Prose tends to overstate its case, whereas poetry by its very nature makes a delicate affirmation which "does not seriously jostle our other beliefs; we can accept its faint breeze of truth without mental inconvenience" [Wheelwright, 1958, p. 95].

aubade: a poem conventionally lamenting the arrival of the day which must separate lovers. In modern poetry, the convention is often used ironically. Ex: "Morning at the Window" (19).

audience: a group of addressees, present during a performance, or implied as a readership. It may be helpful to distinguish between an identifiable small audience, physically present and a mass public.

auditory imagination: "What I call the 'auditory imagination' is the feeling for syllable and rhythm, penetrating far below the conscious levels of thought and feeling, invigorating every word; sinking to the most primitive and forgotten, returning to the origin and bringing something back, seeking the beginning and the end; it works through meanings, certainly, or not without meanings in the ordinary sense, and fuses the old and the obliterated and the trite, the current and the new and the surprising, the most ancient and the most civilized mentality." [Eliot, 1933, p. 118-119].

cadence: the patterning of rhythm in ordinary speech, or in nonmetrical verse. The King James Bible and Walt Whitman's *Leaves of Grass* (1855) use cadenced verse.

caesura: a pause in the line, often marked by some visual sign. The caesura can be initial, medial or terminal.

cento: from the Latin for patchwork, a cento is a collage of verses from other people's work.

chiasmus: a self-enclosing repetition of elements as in the pattern *xyyx*.

comedy of manners: a comedy which questions the code of behaviour of the fashionable part of society, in which appearances are more important than moral character. The comedy depends on verbal wit, and the unscrupulous characters are not punished. Ex: Restoration comedy, the plays of Oscar Wilde, and Eliot's postwar plays. And "Portrait of a Lady"?

composition: the way in which different elements of an artwork are combined or arranged.

coterie: a small gathering of the like-minded. It may be a reading community (Oxford, Garsington) or a writing community (Futurists, Imagists, Surrealists…).

Dadaism: a short-lived nonsensical movement launched in Zurich in 1916. Cf. Tristan Tzara's *Dada Manifesto* (1920).

difficult: troublesome or perplexing, which are not the same things. Of the four sources of difficulty in modern poetry listed by Eliot (s. Introduction), the last is perhaps the most interesting: that the reader may be looking for a prose meaning that is not there.

discordia concors: harmonious discord, when harmony or unity is gained by combining disparate or conflicting elements.

dissociation of sensibility: a theory proposed by Eliot as to what, regrettably, happened to English poetry after the Metaphysical poets, i.e., the separation of thought from feeling. cf. "The poets of the seventeenth century, the successors of the dramatists of the sixteenth, possessed a mechanism of sensibility which could devour any kind of experience. They are simple, artificial, difficult, or fantastic, as their predecessors were; no less nor more than Dante, Guido Cavalcanti, Guinicelli, or Cino. In the seventeenth century a dissociation of sensibility set in, from which we have never recovered; and this dissociation, as is natural, was aggravated by the influence of the two most powerful poets of the century, Milton and Dryden." ("The Metaphysical Poets", 1921).

dramatic monologue: soliloquy in which the addressee is present in the poem but does not speak directly. Ex: Robert Browning's "My Last Duchess".

dream vision: a mediaeval form in which a narrator falls asleep and, often helped by a guide, has an allegorical dream. Lewis Carroll's Alice in Wonderland would be a modern form of dream vision. And "Gerontion"?

dropped line: a line broken into two lines, with the second indented to the place where it would have occurred if the line had not been broken. This is done deliberately by the author, to create a horizontal rhythm, heightening tension. **Dropped** lines are not to be confused with **turnover** lines, which are merely the typesetter's solution to a line that is exceptionally long. For turnover lines the indentation is conventional. Turnover lines are rare in Eliot until "Ash Wednesday", but there is an example on page 60. "Death by Water" (65) is a superb example of the performative* power of dropped lines.

ekphrasis: a vivid description of a scene or a work of art. Ex: The first 33 ll. of "A Game of Chess" (56).

ellipsis: the omission of words whose absence does not prevent our understanding the line. Ellipsis makes a poem more 'difficult', but the concentration gained by elimination adds intensity to the poetic experience.

end: Understanding the word polysemically, Paul Muldoon in *The End of the Poem*, explores the relationship between a poem and its end. What is a poem's end (aim)? How and why do poems end, as opposed to go on and on? An **end-stopped**, as opposed to a run-on, line contains a finished phrase. How does this affect meaning?

enjambment: a sentence which runs over the line length.

epigraph: a quotation from another work placed in italics at the beginning of a work.

free verse: can be distinguished from prose by its use of line forms, and by its greater control of the rhythm of the phrase. Free verse uses for its cohesion cadence, repetition, balancing of visual and auditory rhythm.

Futurism: a movement in Italy and Russia that called for new verse to match the speed and violence of twentieth-century technology. cf. F.T. Marinetti's Futurist manifestos.

Georgian poets: the mainly young, bucolic poets who appeared in the Georgian anthologies (1912-1922) edited by Edward Marsh. They were considered the antithesis of the Modernists, although D.H. Lawrence's poem "Snake" first appeared in these anthologies.

heteronym: a pseudonym created so that an author may write in a different style. Fernando Pessoa (1888-1935) is the best-known theorist and practitioner of this semi-autobiographical device. Although Eliot was more interested in experimenting with a polyphony of voices, rather than the development of the voice of a single persona, it should be remembered that "Portrait of a Lady" was originally titled "Prufrock among the Women".

historical sense: "The historical sense involves a perception, not only of the pastness of the past, but of its presence; the historical sense compels a man to write not merely with his own generation in his bones, but with a feeling that the whole of the literature of Europe from Homer and within it the whole of the literature of his own country has a simultaneous existence and composes a simultaneous order. This historical sense, which is a sense of the timeless as well as of the temporal and of the timeless and of the temporal together, is what makes a writer traditional. And it is at the same time what makes a writer most acutely conscious of his place in time, of his own contemporaneity." ("Tradition and the Individual Talent", 1919).

hypallage: a transferred epithet. Ex: *peevish gutter*, muttering retreats.

hyperbaton: the inversion of the normal order of words. Ex: *Us he devours*.

hyperbole: an extravagant exaggeration from the Greek for 'overshooting', a deliberately exaggerated claim.

image: the mental image created by an appeal to any of the five senses.

Imagism: a transatlantic poetic movement which flourished 1912-1917, under the influence of T.E. Hulme and Ezra Pound.

impersonality: "I like to feel that a writer is perfectly cool and detached, regarding other people's feelings or his own, like a God who has got beyond them; or a person who has dived very deep and comes up holding firmly some hitherto unseen submarine creature," said Eliot in a letter to Mary Hutchinson, 1917. Also "What every poet starts from is his own emotions.... Shakespeare, too, was occupied with the struggle —which alone constitutes life for a poet— to transmute his personal and private agonies into something rich and strange, something universal and impersonal." (Shakespeare and the Stoicism of Seneca", 1927). The author is naturally absent in drama, speaking through the *dramatis personae*.

innuendo: an oblique remark, a hint, or a suggestion.

intermediality: the search for meaning across media.

intertextuality: the making of a connection between literary texts which, unlike allusion, does not rely on the connection having been intended by the author.

invocation: an address to a deity or Muse.

irony: an implied meaning, based on a gap between what is said and what is meant. Its use involves some dissembling on the part of the writer, and implies a certain amount of understatement. **Dramatic irony** is at work when the audience knows more about what is happening than the speaker.

Late Elizabethan dramatists: the dramatists discussed by Eliot (Ben Jonson, Drayton, Beaumont and Fletcher, Webster, Middleton, Massinger) are more often seen as belonging to the Jacobean Age.

line-length: may be measured in feet (tetrameter, pentameter are the most common) or syllables. Often irregular in modern verse.

little magazine: the literary magazines which helped modern poetry and the work of young writers to circulate. Sometimes called 'the shock-troops of Modernism'.

litotes: understatement.

lyric poem: a short poem expresses a state of mind and/or a process of thought.

meaning: according to Eliot's notorious comment, "The chief use of the 'meaning' of a poem, in the ordinary sense, may be (for here again I am speaking of some kinds of poetry and not all) to satisfy one habit of the reader, to keep his mind diverted and quiet, while the poem does its work upon him: much as the imaginary burglar is always provided with a bit of nice meat for the house-dog." [ELIOT, 1933, p. 151].

metaphor: a direct comparison. Metaphors can be extended.

metonymy: a part standing for a whole. Ex: "For all the history of grief / An empty doorway and a maple leaf" (Archibald MacLeish, "Ars poetica", 1926). Of what is 'peach' a metonymy in "Do I dare to eat a peach?" (7).

metre: the use of a regular syllabic stress pattern and a recurrent number of feet in a line. The most common verse meter in English is the iambic pentameter, and even free verse resorts on occasion to metrical feet. The easiest way to remember the main types of metre is to memorize this excerpt from a poem that S.T. Coleridge sent to his son Derwent in 1807:

> Trōchĕe trīps frŏm lōng tŏ shōrt;
> From long to long in solemn sort
> Slōw Spōndēe stālks, strōng fōot!, yet ill able
> Ēvĕr tŏ cōme ŭp wĭth Dāctȳl trĭsȳllăblĕ.
> Ĭāmbĭcs mārch frŏm shōrt tŏ lōng.
> Wĭth ă lēap ănd ă bōund thĕ swĭft Ānăpĕsts thrōng.

Since the **rising rhythm** of iambics and anapests is more common in English poetry than the **falling rhythm** of trochees and dactyls, it is wise to pay attention to the deliberate use of any exception to the general rule. In "Reflections on vers libres", Eliot observes that "the most interesting verse which has yet been written in our language has been done either by taking a very simple form, like the iambic pentameter, and constantly withdrawing from it, or taking no form at all, and constantly approximating to a very simple one. It is this contrast between fixity and flux, this unperceived evasion of monotony, which is the very life of verse." And, to drive his point home, he added, "There is no escape from metre; there is only mastery." [ELIOT, 1965, p. 185].

Modernism: a complex term, conferred retrospectively on the period 1880-1930, involving a break with the traditional foundations of Western thought and culture. Eliot observed that the inherited mode of literary writing assumed a relatively stable social order which was no longer available to the contemporary artist who lived within "the immense panorama of futility and anarchy which is contemporary history". Modernism is often associated with Pound's injunction to "make it new".

motif: a term borrowed from musicology to designate a recurrent feature in a work, a concrete element as opposed to a longer and more abstract **theme**.

negative capability: cf. "at once it struck me what quality went to form a Man of Achievement, especially in Literature, and which Shakespeare possessed so enormously —I mean Negative Capability, that is, when a man is capable of being in uncertainties, mysteries, doubts, without any irritable reaching after fact and reason—" (John Keats, letter to his brothers, 21 December 1817).

objective correlative: a term invented by Eliot himself in "Hamlet" (1919): "The only way of expressing emotion in the form of art is by finding an 'objective correlative'; in other words, a set of objects, a situation, a chain of events which shall be the formula of that particular emotion; such that when the external facts, which must terminate in sensory experience, are given, the emotion is immediately evoked." Eliot is criticizing Shakespeare, but how far does Eliot himself in each poem live up to his own rule?

performative language: From Speech Act Theory, when words *do* what they *say*. In *How to Do things with Words*, J.L. Austin gives the example of "With this ring I thee wed". Robert Graves believed that the central function of the poetic use of language was to be performative: "*Nothing promised that is not performed*".

onomatopoeia: in addition to making one feel good when one has mastered how to spell it, this word designates the mimicry of sound in speech especially, though not only, animal sounds. Ex: In "Reflections on Vers libres" Eliot talks of the "music that has hitherto *chirped* unnoticed in the expanse of prose" [ELIOT, 1965. My emphasis].

paratext: the text that accompanies the literary text (preface, introduction, table of contents, notes, and so on). The epitext are the texts relating to the literary text but published elsewhere, such as reviews, letters, publicity material and so on.

persona: voice created by the poet to be the speaker of the poem. After the Latin word for 'mask'. The 'I' of a modern lyric is rarely the personal utterance of the poet, an autobiographical event. Ex: Prufrock, Gerontion.

personification: one of the principal techniques of allegory.

poetry for poetry's sake: the title of A.C. Bradley's inaugural lecture as Oxford Chair of Poetry, delivered in 1901, published in 1909, in which he affirmed that, "The nature of poetry is to be not a part, nor yet a copy, of the real world (as we commonly understand that phrase), but to be a world by itself, independent, complete, autonomous; and to possess it fully you must enter that world, conform to its laws, and ignore for the time the beliefs, aims, and particular conditions which belong to you in the other world of reality."

polysemy: a figure of speech which releases the forces of latent meaning, and paradox. Ex: 'sense' signposts the sensual and intellectual faculties which, acting together, constitute meaning.

Post-impressionism: a term first used by Roger Fry in 1906, and then again when he organized the 1910 exhibition *Manet and the Post-Impressionists*, defining it as the development of French art since Édouard Manet. It now refers to the French art of 1886-1914. The first exhibition of 1910-11 focussed on the work of Paul Cézanne, Paul Gauguin, Georges Seurat and Vincent van Gogh. A second exhibition in 1912 featured the work of Henri Matisse and Pablo Picasso.

prose-poem: a well-crafted short prose passage which would convey the *frisson* of poetry. Baudelaire called for "a poetic prose, musical without rhyme, supple and agile enough to adapt to the lyrical movements of the mind".

rhyme: see the "Rhyme" chapter.

rhyme pattern, rhyme scheme: seldom present in Eliot's verse, except in the quatrain poems.

satire: often divided into two types: the gentle Horatian (Horace, Dryden, Pope) and the sardonic Juvenalian (Juvenal, Dr. Johnson, Byron)

significant form: term used by art critic Clive Bell in *Art* (1914) to describe the potential in a work of art to provoke an emotional response in the viewer.

simile: *Collected Poems* begins with a simile: *When the evening is spread out against the sky / Like a patient etherized upon a table;* In what ways exactly are evening and artificially induced unconsciousness similar? Perhaps both are moments of surrender to the unknown? Simile, long neglected in favour of metaphor and metonymy, is currently the focus of critical interest. cf. A.E. Stallings' poetry collection *Like* (2018) and Alice Oswald's beautiful image of the "lattice-work of likeness" in "Manifesto" (2023). In that lecture she also made a mock-appeal for a new poetic movement: 'similism'.

soliloquy: the act of talking aloud to oneself, in the absence of anyone to hear. It is mainly used in drama. E.g., in *Hamlet* but also in "Gerontion". J.S. Mill thought that the presence or absence of an actual or ideal listener separated rhetoric from poetry: "Poetry and eloquence are both alike the expression or utterance of feeling: but, if we may be excused the antithesis, we should say that eloquence is *heard*; poetry is *over*heard. Eloquence supposes an audience. The peculiarity of poetry appears to us to lie in the poet's utter unconsciousness of a listener. Poetry is feeling confessing itself to itself in moments of solitude, and embodying itself in symbols which are the nearest possible representations of the feeling in the exact shape in which it exists in the poet's mind. Eloquence is feeling pouring itself out to other minds, courting their sympathy, or endeavoring to influence their belief, or move them to passion or to action." ("Thoughts on Poetry and its Varieties", 1833).

Symbolism: "a literature in which the visible world is no longer a reality, and the unseen world no longer a dream" [SYMONS, 1919, p. 4]. The best way to understand what 'symbolism' meant to Eliot is to read the introduction to Symons' study.

tableau vivant: a silent and motionless group of people arranged to represent a scene. The allusion in the title of "A Game of Chess" is a powerful example: it is to the scene in *The Tempest* (V, 1) where Prospero draws back the curtain to show Miranda and Ferdinand silently playing chess. We are thus given to understand that the whole play is indeed 'play'.

theme: an extended and multifaceted *motif*. A few examples of themes one might find in Eliot's early poetry: alienation, dislocation, *ennui*, ritual and romance, the sacred and the profane, uncertainty…

title: an element of a poem that is too often neglected. All of Eliot's published poems have titles, but no sections of his poems do. To what extent, and how, does the title of a poem guide our reading of that poem? What is the difference between *The Wasteland* and *The Waste Land*? What would happen if *The Waste Land* were retitled *The Vision of Tiresias* (72)?

tone: conveys the speaker's attitude to what is being said. In a letter to Lytton Strachey in 1919, Eliot draws attention to the importance, for him, of tone: "Whether one writes a piece of work well or not seems to me a matter of crystallization — the good sentence, the good word, is only the final stage in the process. One can groan over the choice of a word, but there is something much more important to groan over first. It seems to me just the same in poetry — the work comes easily enough, in comparison to the core of it —the tone— and nobody can help in the least with that." [ELIOT, 1988, p. 298]

vers libres: in "Reflections on Vers libres" (1917) Eliot professes an antipathy to free verse: "If *vers libre* is a genuine verse-form it will have a positive definition. And I can define it only in negatives: (1) absence of pattern, (2) absence of rhyme, (3) absence of metre." In the rest of this masterly essay, he goes on to show why there can be no freedom in art. [ELIOT, 1965, p. 184].

verse paragraph: a group of lines forming a unit which is determined by the sense rather than stanza form.

voice: the characteristics displayed by the speaker of the poem, inferred from their tone, style, and perspective.

worldview: "the most ordinary beliefs about the constitution of the world" [TILLYARD, 1943, p. viii]. The prejudices of our times affect the demands which we as readers, make on poetry, and these are aesthetic limitations, or prejudices, which can be historically explained.

zeugma: the grammatical yoking together of two unlike words.

Éditions Atlande
F - 92200 Neuilly
www.Atlande.eu

Achevé d'imprimer sur les presses de la Sepec Numérique
à Peronnas (Ain) en novembre 2023.
Numéro d'impression : N10017230913

Dépôt légal décembre 2023.

PEFC 10-31-3532 IMPRIM'VERT®